W9-CAT-607

Making Peace
With Your
Inner
Child

RITA BENNETT

Fleming H. Revell
A Division of Baker Book House
Grand Rapids, Michigan 49506

The accounts in this book are factual; however, to protect confidentiality, some of the names of people and identifying details have been changed. In these instances, any resemblance to persons living or dead is purely coincidental.

Library of Congress Cataloging-in-Publication Data

Bennett, Rita.
   Making peace with your inner child.
   Bibliography: p.
   1. Christian life—Anglican authors.   2. Spiritual healing.
   I. Title.
BV4501.2.B3928   1987   248.4'83   86-31370
ISBN 0-8007-5240-6

Copyright © 1987 by Rita Bennett
Published by Fleming H. Revell
a division of Baker Book House Company
P.O. Box 6287, Grand Rapids, Michigan 49516-6287

Fifth printing, November 1992

Printed in the United States of America

THIS BOOK IS LOVINGLY DEDICATED
TO MY FATHER, WILLIAM HARVEY REED,
AND MY MOTHER, LORETTA ELLEN REED (*both departed*)
for whom I am most grateful and whom I honor

Contents

Introduction

In a contemporary world that promises peace but never really gives it, the subject of finding peace needs to be looked at again. We know why people without Christ don't have peace, but why don't Christians consistently live in the "peace that passes understanding" promised by Scripture? Then, too, when we are at peace, we almost feel guilty, since at the same time the news media show that many people in the world are miserable and in distress!

Jesus gave us two viewpoints on peace. When He foretold the persecution at hand He said, "Do not think that I came to bring peace on earth. I did not come to bring peace but a sword" (Matthew 10:34). When He talked about division coming because of the Gospel He said, "Do you suppose that I came to give peace on earth? I tell you, not at all, but rather division" (Luke 12:51).

But to God's children He speaks differently; He promises us the gift of peace. He says it's our heritage. Before His death Jesus said, "Peace I leave with you, My peace I give to you; not as the world gives do I give to you. Let not your heart be troubled, neither let it be afraid" (John 14:27). Later, close to His arrest in Gethsemane He said, "I have told you all this so that in me you may find peace. In the world you will have trouble. But courage! The victory is mine; I have conquered the world" (John 16:33 NEW ENGLISH BIBLE).

But what is this *peace* which we speak of so glibly? There are dif-

ferent ways to describe this quality of life. I'll list several that apply
to the meaning used in this book as given in *Webster's New Colle-
giate Dictionary* (1980).

> a state of tranquillity or quiet;
>
> *tranquil:* free from disturbance or turmoil;
>
> free from agitation of mind or spirit;
>
> freedom from disquieting or oppressive thoughts or emo-
> tions;
>
> harmony in personal relationships.

Obviously God intends the child of God to be able to live in
peace, even with turmoil looming all around. We somehow have to
find the calm in the midst of the storm. Our center is ". . . Christ in
you, the hope of glory" (Colossians 1:27).

I believe that in the resurrected human spirit, which is joined to
the Lord, *the peace of God resides.* The difficulty is in getting God's
peace to flow as a river from this center of God's life within our
spirits, into our wills, intellects, emotions, motivational life, and
into and out through our bodies to others. The ultimate goal is to
have the *"peace that passes"* not only understanding, but passes on to
others.

This is what *Making Peace With Your Inner Child* is about. Soul-
healing prayer is an important way in which God is healing the
wounds of His people so they can *pass on the peace of God.* It isn't the
only way for such healing to take place, but it's most effective, and
continues to amaze and bless me.

Making Peace With Your Inner Child is actually the third in a tril-
ogy of inner-healing books I've written. The first was *Emotionally
Free,* a primer on the subject. The second, *How to Pray for Inner
Healing for Yourself and Others,* helps the layperson, as well as the
pastor or counselor, help himself and others. The third, the present
book, takes a deeper look at parent-child relationships, gives several

in-depth prayer sessions and case studies, and a solid foundation for establishing inner and outer peace. With prayers interspersed throughout, you, the reader, will be guided to pray through your own needs.

I think you will find these three books more effective if read in sequence, as each builds on the other.

It is highly rewarding to receive testimonies from those helped by the books. Abortions have been stopped, suicides prevented, marriages saved, homosexuals given hope and healing, and families reconciled. Prisoners in the USA and England have accepted Jesus and been healed. I'll borrow some words from the lovely gospel song written by Fanny Crosby, "To God be the glory—great things He hath done!"

This book, like my others, encourages laypeople to get involved. I suggest you read and *study* all three, to prepare yourself before launching out. It would also help if you attend a seminar and work on a prayer team, and follow this by working with a church which offers this ministry.

Much of my preparation for the work God opened up was in the school of life. After I graduated from college, I taught elementary school for several years; then worked one year with psychologists rehabilitating emotionally disturbed children. Following this, I taught exceptional children for a year, and then spent several years as a child-welfare social worker in adoption studies, foster care, and juvenile detention. The Lord has a wonderful way of using our backgrounds, whatever they may be. He will make use of yours also.

I'll close these introductory thoughts with my prayer for you:

PRAYER FOR PEACE

Dear Lord, Prince of Peace,
when You walked this earth You spoke peace to your creation,
the wind and waves,
and to Your people Your usual greeting was
"Shalom—Peace be unto you."
You taught Your disciples it was a gift they could impart;
it was a tangible kind of peace.

Lord Jesus Christ,
may Your peace rest upon this book
and those who read it.
Walk to us on the waves
of turmoil and agitation around us.
Let us hear You
speak the command, "Peace, be still."

Come aboard our ship, Lord,
to still the thunder of the storms within *our souls,*
as well as without.
Free us from disquieting or oppressive thoughts and emotions.
Be our Tranquillity.
Bring us into wholeness and complete integration.
Be our Counselor. Our Reconciler.

As we live our lives in fellowship with You,
Oh, Blesser of peacemakers,
teach us to enter into the rest that only You can give.
Guide our ship into the waterways that are right for us,
and when it's time,
bring us safely to shore.
Amen. So be it.

RITA BENNETT

Acknowledgments

I wish to thank the people quoted in this book for allowing me to share their inspiration and witness. May God, through them, bless and heal multitudes.

Thanks to my friends at the office, Cory Phillips, Robbi Allen, and Florence Dressel, who prayed consistently for me and this book. That also includes many other prayer partners, and friends at home and abroad.

My special thanks and abundant appreciation to my husband, Dennis, for his constant love and support in every way, and his contributions to the book.

Many thanks to those who took time from their busy schedules to read and advise me on my book: to John Rodgers, Bill and Barbara Frey, and Karl and Joyce Strader. And to those at Fleming H. Revell who took time to read and encourage me.

Most of all, thanks be to God!

Chapter One

Making Peace With Your Hurt Inner Child

"Blessed are the peacemakers:
For they shall be called the children of God."
Matthew 5:9
The words of Jesus Christ

CALLED AND CHOSEN

O little child,
set in the midst of Jesus, and His disciples.
Imagine the glory you felt,
the love surrounding you—
the peace
that must have filled your little being.

Your smile must have stretched for miles.
Little did you know this glorious morn that you awoke,
He would choose you,
of all the followers, of all the children,
to sit with Him, the Master of the Universe.

Surely, from the beginning of time,
He knew your name,
He called you, He chose you
and now this day;
filled with sunshine, the singing of birds,
He has called you,
loved you,
set you apart.

VAL JOHANSEN SOHM
based on Matthew 18:1–4

Nearly three thousand years ago Isaiah said: "The wolf also shall dwell/with the lamb, The leopard shall lie down/with the young goat, The calf and the young lion/and the fatling together; And a little child shall lead them" (Isaiah 11:6).

This verse and the rest of the chapter speak about the "Day of the Lord" when at His return all the world will be *peaceful,* including the animal kingdom. Most of us are reminded of this each Christmas when we get at least one Christmas card with a picture of the "Peaceable Kingdom," a lion lying down with a lamb.

But do we need to wait until then to walk in God's peace? Christians are in one sense living in the "Day of the Lord" now.

What does it mean, "A little child shall lead them"?

First of all, Jesus came to earth as a vulnerable little Child, so He could take us by the hand, bring us back to God, and give us His everlasting life and peace. His coming, death, Resurrection, Ascension, and sending of the Holy Spirit are the great Good News, and *the foundation for all the outer and inner peace I will be telling you about.*

This Scripture can have other meanings. I have known of children who have taken their parents by the hand and led them to Jesus. I've known children to lead adults in other ways. There was a feature story on the Christian Broadcasting Network, Inc., in 1984, about an eleven-year-old boy in Philadelphia who led his church and many people in the city to show love to the "down and outers" who made their homes on the streets. Instead of having them come to a shelter for help, Trevor Ferrell went to them where they were living, under a newspaper, with a bench for a bed or a curb for a pillow. He urged others to this "love in action," and they began to take food, blankets, pillows, and other helpful items to the destitute, and showed as well as told them about Jesus' love. The name *Philadelphia* is from the Greek word meaning brotherly love, and this love was certainly shown through this child, his parents, and the church who believed in him enough to back up his ideas.[1]

Another Way of Looking at Isaiah 11:6

Still another way of looking at this Scripture is to see it speaking about your own inner child. Within you is both a child and an adult. This is true both scripturally and psychologically.

I told about the inner child in my two previous books on soul-healing prayer. Let's briefly review a few of the concepts. What is your inner child? It is the interior record of your emotions and memories during the first five or six years of your life, *including your prenatal life.*

There are two types of the inner child, I call them:

The Creative Child

The Hurt Child

The Creative Child is made up of all the healed and healthy attitudes and memories of your early life that help you be:

open
loving
quick to forgive

trusting
imaginative
spontaneous
creative
playful
inquisitive
unaffected
free
willing to try new things
responsive.

Through the Holy Spirit working in one's life these attributes can be strengthened, or through hurts in life they can be diminished. What I'm calling the "Creative Child" within is what I believe Jesus was talking about when He said, ". . . unless you are converted, and become as little children, you will by no means enter the kingdom of heaven" (Matthew 18:3). Trusting God takes childlike simplicity, and that's why Jesus wanted you and me to become as little children.

It seems paradoxical that Jesus says He wants you to be childlike, while at the same time Paul says in his letter to the Ephesians that you should be maturing, growing up (Ephesians 4:15). Both instructions are equally important, and if it weren't possible to do both, God wouldn't have told you to.

Jesus had these two qualities and kept them in balance. No believer would doubt that Jesus was the most mature person who ever lived, yet not everyone would be sure of His childlikeness. Jesus Himself said, "The Son can do nothing by himself. He does only what he sees the Father doing, and in the same way" (John 5:19 TLB).

The Hurt Child is made up of the unhealed attitudes, memories, and reactions to those memories which sometimes cause us to regress to negative childhood behavior. The more injured a person is, the more often he will find himself feeling and acting like this Hurt Child. The childish adult at times may:

throw temper tantrums to get control
pout
speak in a childish whiny voice
cry to get his way
throw things
be extremely self-centered
think the world revolves around him
look for someone to blame for his problems
avoid responsibility
run away from home and problems (or want to)
often be afraid of his own peers
resist change
have a great sense of inadequacy
be too frightened to speak in public
take refuge in fantasy.

Jesus said, ". . . Let the little children come to Me, and do not forbid them; for of such is the kingdom of God" (Mark 10:14). As you know, when Jesus said this He was encouraging parents to bring their children to Him so He could bless them. Yet you can also hear Him saying to you that He wants you to bring your own *Creative* Inner Child to Him for His blessing, and that He also wants you to bring your *Hurt* Inner Child with its emptiness, need for love, traumas, and neglect to Him, so He can pick that child up and hold him or her close in His healing arms. He wants to transform your Hurt Child.

First Corinthians 13:11 says, "When I was a child, I spoke as a child, I understood as a child; I thought as a child; but when I became a man [an adult], I put away childish things." Child*ish* behavior is very different from child*like* behavior. Childish behavior must be put away, but saying it is so much easier than doing it. *Recognizing the need, however, brings helpful diagnosis and prayer is the cure.*

This you will experience as you read further.

The Wounds of Jeremiah and Moses

In these accounts you see that Jeremiah and Moses suffered from inadequacies which sometimes sent them back to feeling like hurt children.

When Jeremiah was a young man, God told him He had known him from the time of his conception, and that before he was born, He had called him to serve as a prophet. Jeremiah's response was something like this: "I can't speak for you Lord: I'm only a child [he was actually a teenager]" (see Jeremiah 1:6f). Then God spoke strongly to him, lifted him out of his inadequate child, and told him He would enable him to do the work he was called to. This is what God wants to do for every one of us. We only need to trust enough to risk saying, "Yes, Lord." He can then show us the way, and give us the power and love we need.

So Jeremiah went out in faith to a ministry which was not exactly popular. He tells about it in chapter 20 of his prophecies: "For I heard the defaming of many, fear on every side. Report, say they, and we will report it. All my familiars watched for my halting. . . . But the Lord is with me as a mighty terrible one: therefore my persecutors shall stumble, and they shall not prevail: they shall be greatly ashamed; for they shall not prosper . . ." (v. 10,11 KJV). But even after these confident words, Jeremiah goes on to bemoan his birth, "Cursed be the day wherein I was born: let not the day my mother bare me be blessed" (v. 14). He begins to let his hurts control his life. He stops speaking from the spirit, and speaks from the hurts in his soul, which possibly went back to his early childhood.

In chapter 4 of Exodus, God calls another man, Moses, to lead the children of Israel out of slavery and into the Land of Promise. Moses responded to the Lord, ". . . I am slow of speech, and of a slow tongue" (v.10). Moses spent a long time trying to convince God that he was not the right man for the job. (Read vv. 1–17.) This is not surprising if you remember Moses' difficult beginning. Pharaoh had decreed all Hebrew males be killed at birth. Moses' mother put him on a little raft which she hid among the tall reeds along the bank of the Nile. Pharaoh's daughter found baby Moses and wanted to keep him. Moses' sister (who *happened* to be standing near), conveniently offered to find a nurse for him, his own mother. He had her care and love for a while longer.

Eventually Moses was taken from his parents' home to Pharaoh's palace (Moses is the first adopted child the Scriptures record). It may sound glamorous to be adopted by a princess, but he would still have felt rejected by his parents because the infant Moses would not have understood. I'm speculating, but I believe some of these problems helped give Moses his feelings of inadequacy and perhaps the speech impediment he writes about.

The Theme

"A little child shall lead them." Isaiah 11:6 pictures a fearless and whole child who, through the Lord, is growing into full potential, becoming a true leader.

You can see this in your own inner child, and can be encouraged to know that *if you put your hand in Jesus' hand,* He can lead your inner child to wholeness, and then, if needed, your inner child will be able to help lead your adult-self into wholeness. When you understand your inner child and what happened to him or her in the past, missing pieces of the puzzle will fall into place. As your child and adult are reconciled, you will truly become whole and will understand better how to bring wholeness to others.

Unless you make peace with this hurt child-self within—a part of you that you've perhaps rejected and even despised—you will not become whole the way God wants you to. These hurts cannot keep you from heaven, but may limit what God can do through you in this life.

Leanne Payne, a former research fellow at Yale Divinity School says: "When the real person isn't allowed to live, all kinds of strange behavior patterns can emerge." I believe the real person

Leanne speaks of here is not only who you are now but who you have been from your beginning.

Why Pray About Childhood?

In soul-healing, we pray about our entire life: past, present, and future. Childhood is one of the most important times to pray about, because it's foundational. For some people, prenatal life and infancy are even more important, but since we don't remember those times, it's usually best to begin praying about conscious memories. God will bring to mind other things we need to pray about as we go along. Through our faith and experience as Christians, some of these childhood hurts will have already been healed, yet all of us are different and have to determine the need for further healing individually. As I've said so often, "Every experience with Jesus brings inner healing; therefore, every Christian has already received some inner healing."

John Powell, author and priest, says about childhood, "Although it is difficult to accept, the psychological scars that we have acquired during these first seven years remain in some way with us for life. No very deep psychological problems originate after this age, although these scars and scar tissue may be aggravated or inflamed by circumstances occurring later in our lives . . . We are each of us, the product of those who have loved us . . . or refused to love us.[2]

Reconciliation With Ourselves

You may need reconciliation between your adult and child-selves so you can grow. Your adult may need to ask your inner child to forgive you for ignoring it (and sometimes so hating it that you don't want to acknowledge it ever existed or exists now). On the other hand, your inner child may need to ask your adult to forgive it for dragging its feet and not letting him or her reach full growth and full potential.

I recall praying a prayer of reconciliation for a man who didn't like his child-self. When he was a child he was not allowed to be a child: to think, act, and talk like a child. He had had to put away his childhood too early (1 Corinthians 13:11). His mother rejected the emotional side of life but stressed and approved the intellectual. He was brighter than most of the other kids, and his mother's attitude caused him to separate from his peers even more. He was directed to be a little, intellectual, old man while still a child.

As we prayed about his blocked emotions, I was led to ask if he could remember a park where he had gone in his childhood. Every child has been to a park at some time, and he was no exception. He said, "Yes, I can remember a park. In fact I can picture it clearly. I must have been six or seven at the time."

"Since the Bible teaches God is omnipresent during our entire lifetime," I said, "God must have been with you at that age even though you perhaps weren't aware of Him.[3] Could you by faith see Jesus there in the park and let Him love and comfort you?"

He said he'd try. As he closed his eyes to pray, he could picture Jesus walking along with him, holding his hand as they walked and talked together.

After he had had a chance to enjoy this time with Jesus, I felt I should ask, "Can you picture yourself now, as an adult, joining Jesus and the boy in the park?"

He was quiet awhile and then said, "I can, but I'd rather be alone with Jesus and not have the child there. I guess I have a problem with him." After praying further, he could allow himself as an adult to go to the park.

He was happy to see Jesus but still not happy to see the boy. I felt Jesus, the Reconciler, wanted to put His arms around both the adult and child, but my friend couldn't experience this. I then asked him, "Can you hug the boy?"

He answered, "No . . . but I've reached out to hold his hand. But this isn't enough," he said. "Jesus is asking me to kiss the child and . . . I'm doing it!" A sob escaped from him.

The Holy Spirit began to move freely from there, and when my friend could speak, he described how the scene became happy and free; Jesus had put the boy on His shoulders and the three of them went for a walk. More time elapsed, and when God's work was completed, we thanked Him for His healing love and guidance during our prayer.

I learned this capsule truth that day: If you have unhealed hurts from your childhood and are very resistant to the idea of praying about those memories (especially if you can't stand that little kid of the past), you need healing prayer.

Another Example

In the spring of 1981, Jenny[4] had been going through a trying period because a close friend had decided not to be "best" friends anymore. This would be difficult for anyone, but it was upsetting to Jenny beyond a normal reaction. She had been grieving many months and had lost quite a bit of weight. Jenny detected by her symptoms that she needed help and asked a friend and me for prayer.

Jenny shared some of her childhood memories with us, and we saw the root cause of her overreaction was she felt abandoned because of hurts during infancy.

Jenny explained, "I was a much-wanted child and much celebrated at my birth. It was a happy beginning until I was four months old, and my older sister became seriously ill. Her health problem lasted about fourteen months. During the first month, our parents nearly had to live at the hospital. Even when my sister came home, Mother had to tend her most of the time."

We began praying with *adult* Jenny by helping her say she accepted *little* Jenny. (A similar prayer to the boy in the park.) She told her it was okay to be highly celebrated at birth. Big Jenny gave little Jenny much love and she said she felt as though the little child was in her arms.

Then little Jenny said she accepted big Jenny with all the hurts, reservations, and fears she had accumulated. She gave grown-up

Jenny the unreserved, unspoiled love she had received during her first four months. It was pure healing love.

We then prayed about the scene where at four months Jenny felt abandoned. As she remembered, she felt the hurt deeply and cried out. She didn't realize how much it had hurt. We prayed for her release from feeling abandoned and from fearing such experiences in the future. She then saw Jesus, the ever-present Lord, come to her crib and cup her face in His hands, and say, ". . . I will never leave you . . ." (Hebrews 13:5).

So little Jenny offered her anger to Jesus. It was real anger, because a baby of four months doesn't understand sickness, parental responsibility, or how a situation can change suddenly from great comfort to great loss. Also the magnifying glass of a child's mind makes the hurts much greater. She offered to God her anger toward her mother, father, and sister. As she prayed, she realized that her father had been more fearful about the sister's condition than had her mother, who had had confidence everything would be all right. Jenny spoke forgiveness: "Mama, through Jesus I forgive you. I won't hold this against you. I let the hurt go. Jesus is healing me." She forgave the other family members in the same way.

The Lord let her know that He would be her *support system,* and, in fact, had been so from her conception to the present day.

Rate Yourself

After hearing of these two people you may wonder about your own needs. Here are some questions to ask yourself to check how you feel about your own child-self. They will help you see if you will benefit from the soul-healing prayer at the end of this chapter for the integration of your inner child and adult. (Some people will find this prayer more helpful than others.)

 a) I don't like my inner child; I don't like that little kid. I don't want to think about him, much less tell someone else about him (or her)._____(yes, no)

b) I don't want to get acquainted with the child of my past. My past is over and I don't want to remember it any-more._____(yes, no)

c) I feel sorry for my inner child but I do like him. It makes me feel sad when I think of him (or her). _____(yes, no)

d) Not all the time, but most of the time, my inner child feels worthy and approved of. I don't mind talking about this part of my life._____(yes, no)

e) I had a very happy and satisfying childhood and know God approved of me in the past and approves of me now. I enjoy sharing things about my childhood. _____(yes, no)

If the answer is yes:

a) This person is much in need of healing.

b) This person is repressing hurts and needs help.

c) This person would benefit by some healing and affirming prayer.

d) He's in pretty good shape. Could use some soul-healing prayer from time to time.

e) He or she is doing just great.

(*d* and especially *e* would be able to help someone else in need.)

The Reconciler

I'm teaching about Christian healing, and it's supremely impor-tant, first, that you accept the only One who can truly heal you, Jesus Christ, the Son of God. He is the Reconciler of God and man (Romans 5:18, 19). When you invite Him into your life you are reconciled to God as your sins are forgiven and God, who has always been with you, now comes to live *within* you. You will have received everlasting life.

First, if you have never received Jesus Christ, or are not sure you have, *do it right now.* Turn to Appendix A in the back of the book and use the "Prayer for Receiving Jesus." (If you've already received Jesus into your life, then continue reading.)

Second, if you have been searching for answers in the cults or occult *and have never renounced those things,* before you go on in this prayer and those following in other chapters, turn to Appendix B in the back of the book and pray the "Prayer for Renouncing the Cults and Occult."

God's Presence is both an inner and outer experience. When praying for others for physical healing, I've found the most effective prayer occurs when you have faith within and have built up that faith, and when you also have a person with faith praying for you. Here you have faith *within,* and faith *without.*

Your most solid and important experience is knowing God has come to dwell *inside* you; this brings an inner knowing and confidence deep within your spirit that nothing can compare with. Yet, practicing God's Presence *with* you is also valuable because it allows you to experience His love from the time of your conception, throughout your life, even before you received Jesus' life within as Savior.

As you practice God's Presence in both these directions, you are on the way to making peace within. Your Hurt Inner Child will come into wholeness and will begin to have the attributes of the Creative Child that Jesus wants you to have. Each prayer will bring you further to that goal.

That's what happened to Marty in the next chapter . . .

Soul-Healing Reflection, Prayer, and Evaluation

(Please note: Read through the following Reflection and Prayer, taking time as you go. You may want to read and pray through it again later on when you have more time. If your answer was *e*, or perhaps *d*, you may choose after reading through the prayer to go right to the next chapter.)

Reflection. Call to mind what you looked like at five or six years of age. Think of what you might have been wearing at that time when you went on an outing to a park, or a playground.

Jesus is your omnipresent Lord and has been with you from the very beginning of your life. He loves you dearly. He loves you more than anyone has or ever will. He accepts you just as you are. You are special to Him; close your eyes and take some time to savor His love. You can trust His love for you completely. Take time here to enjoy yourself with Jesus. Let Jesus reacquaint you with this child of your past. (*Pause here.*)

As you let the Holy Spirit direct you, see in what way God will choose to bring together the adult you, and your inner child. It may be like the illustrations given earlier, or in some other way. If you're having trouble with your childhood memories, you may need to take time to talk to Jesus about it. The prayers in each chapter will help you as you go along, or you may want to skip a prayer and come back to it later. (*Pause here.*)

Reconciling Inner Child and Adult Prayer. When ready, picture your *adult and child being reconciled* by Jesus in whatever way He shows you. (*Pause.*)

Say to your inner child: "Through Jesus, I allow you to live and grow into wholeness. I choose to accept you and allow you to be healed. I will stop judging you. Because of Jesus' forgiveness, He has enabled me to forgive you. Let's walk hand in hand with Him."

Take some time to let Jesus bless you with His Presence and bring you His peace. (*Pause here. Take your time.*)

Reconciling child to adult, your inner child may say to your adult-self: "I have disliked you for your weaknesses and mistakes. These things have hurt me and made me not want to grow. With Jesus' help, I choose to let these hurts go and will not hold them against you any longer. Because Jesus has forgiven me, I can forgive and love you."

Feel the peace of Jesus surround you. Know that you're becoming a whole person. The child and adult within are becoming one in Him.

Jesus, while He was on earth, prayed to His Father for us, "I do not pray for these alone, but also for those who will believe in Me through their word; that they all may all be one, as You, Father, are in Me, and I in You; that they also may be one in Us, that the world may believe that You sent Me" (John 17:20, 21). *As you walk in oneness with God and with yourself,* you will be a witness to the world so that they too will believe in Jesus Christ.

Take time to rejoice in your oneness in Christ. Thank God for what He's done in helping you accept yourself more fully and grow in Him. Ask Him how you can share this love with others. (*Pause here.*)

Evaluation. Did your inner child need to accept your adult-self or *vice versa?* Which helped most? You may want to go over this prayer again or have an experienced person pray with you further.[5]

If you found yourself regressing to negative childhood patterns, consider what incident caused your feeling of hurt and inadequacy, and pray you will become aware of the pattern involved for future reference. Reflect on the scene of your little child-self putting his (or her) hand in Jesus' hand so He can lead you to wholeness. You can trust that where He leads you will be good and will make you happiest.

If you couldn't picture yourself as a child, don't be concerned. You don't have to be a visual person to be healed. Some people receive more easily from the Lord through *hearing* Him. Many have lost these creative childlike qualities and need to ask the Lord to restore them. Whether God speaks to you through inspired hearing or picturing, check everything by the Scriptures.

Perhaps you need healing in your self-identity before you can enter into creative praying. If you have this need you may find it difficult even to picture what you yourself are like, and especially how you appear to others. Your self-identity will be healed with time and prayer.

Chapter Two

Marty Makes
Peace With Martha

I will hear what God the Lord will speak:
For He will speak peace
To His people, and to His saints;
But let them not turn back to folly.
Surely His salvation is near to those who fear Him,
That glory may dwell in our land.
Mercy and truth have met together;
Righteousness
and peace
have kissed each other.

Psalms 85:8–10

Peace is the fruit
that grows on the tree
of righteousness.

WILLIAM C. FREY
Episcopal Bishop of Colorado

On a lovely June day in Seattle my phone rang, and I picked it up, delighted to hear the voice of a dear friend. "Barb, it's so good to hear from you!"

"Hello, Rita. I heard you'd be speaking at the Exodus Conference in San Francisco, and I have a friend who is greatly in need of prayer. She's planning to come to the meetings. Marty[1] has had an identity problem since childhood, and a homosexual life-style in the past. She wants to make a complete 'exodus' from her old orientation and wants victory over homosexual feelings and mind-set. I know you'll like her; she's a fine person and a college teacher."

I hesitated a moment, realizing how heavy my schedule would be at a five-day conference. I also realized one prayer time for such deep needs wouldn't be enough. I'd need at least two or three sessions, and even then complete healing for identity problems, barring an outright miracle, could take several years. But at least I could begin! "Sure, Barb," I said. "Ask Marty to introduce herself early in the week, so I can plan my schedule."

Sunday, June 30, my husband, Dennis, and I arrived at San Francisco State University where the conference was to be held. We met with some of the other speakers at registration, found our rooms, and settled in. Exodus is a Christian organization which "seeks to . . . effectively communicate the message of liberation from homosexuality. . . ."[2]

At breakfast next day, Marty found us in the crowd and introduced herself. She was cute and petite; a curly-headed brunette with soft hazel eyes. We enjoyed talking to her, and hearing about her life since she had come to know Jesus personally at age twenty-four. I found her to be motivated and capable; most of her education had been made possible by scholarships and loans that enabled her to graduate and get into a Ph.D. program in psychology in the late sixties. I estimated she must now be in her late thirties, although she looked much younger.

We had a leisurely breakfast and visit. Before leaving I said to Marty, "I don't know if you already have plans for the workshops you'll be attending this week; but if not, I'd like you to consider coming to mine on Prenatal Prayer, Tuesday afternoon. I believe it could be foundational to our time together during the next few days."

"I did have another plan," Marty responded, "but I'll work it out another way. I'll be there!"

"Good," I replied. "Then let's begin our prayer sessions Wednesday morning."

I was glad to see a fine turnout for the workshop, as people with sexual identity problems normally find praying for the beginning stages of their lives very important. In fact, I like to pray for people's sexual identities specifically during the second month of gestation because that's when their bodies first reveal sexual characteristics; the time of birth is also significant because the baby is often accepted or rejected then. The photographer Lennart Nilson, took amazing photographs of prenatal babies beginning at twenty-six days of life.[3] Their sexual characteristics could be seen at the end of the second prenatal month.

Prayer for prenatal and natal life is questioned by some critics who doubt children can think and feel prenatally, or even until the ages of one or two. An article by the well-known Dr. Thomas Verny, in the *Canadian Family Physician* magazine, shows that such criticisims are based on outdated neurological findings.[4]

Some stayed after for group prayer, and Marty was among them. I hoped this would be useful for our praying together the next day. For now, I needed to ask God to send me a prayer partner. (I'm a strong believer in the value of two working together as a team.) Dennis couldn't help as he would be busy with his own ministry.

Prayer One

Walking to breakfast Wednesday morning I still didn't know who God would provide to be my partner about an hour from then, but I was sure He had heard my request. As the saying goes, "God is seldom on time but never late." I caught sight of an attractive blond woman standing at the door of the cafeteria. I found she was waiting to meet us. She introduced herself as Pat Lindstrom, and I found she was a newly licensed marriage and family therapist. After talking with her a few minutes, I felt she was the Lord's choice, and asked if she would be free to work with me. She agreed right away. I sent up an arrow prayer, "Thank You, Lord."

We met Marty at her room later that morning. I could tell by the opening remarks this was going to be a good threesome. We sat down in a small circle, two on a beige dorm hide-a-bed couch and one on a straight-backed metal chair, and spent five or ten minutes visiting and getting acquainted; I asked Marty how the class and prayer time had affected her the previous afternoon.

She said, "As you prayed us through the nine months of development before birth, I could see my beginning as holy, and found I liked myself as a little girl at the second prenatal month. Then in the third month all went fuzzy and hazy. I couldn't pray further."

"That's helpful, Marty," I replied. "It lets me know that your hurts begin very early. Can you fill us in on what was going on in your parents' lives during your mother's pregnancy?"

"My mother became pregnant shortly after my father came home from the war in Europe," she said. "He did not feel financially ready to have a child at that time, but my mother wanted one right away. When he realized a baby was on the way, he decided he wanted a boy, though he was happy with a girl when I arrived. I was given the name *Martha,* though as the years went by I was called by my nickname, *Marty,* which my mother gave me."

"You know, Marty," I ventured, "perhaps we need to go back to prenatal time and pray some more. There's much scriptural precedent for God to intervene during those formative days. Both Isaiah and Jeremiah said God called them 'from the womb'. [Isaiah 44:1, 2; Jeremiah 1:5]. Isaiah even said God had made mention of his name before birth [Isaiah 49:1]. God was there at your beginning too, you know." I smiled at her as I reached for her hand.

Finding Direction for Prayer

The three of us joined hands, and I asked Pat to pray. She thanked God for bringing us together, asked Him to bless us and give clear guidance. I prayed Marty would experience God's love and acceptance from the very beginning of her life. We then waited for the Holy Spirit to lead.

Marty said, "I'm thinking about how Isaiah heard God call his name before he was even born, but when I think about myself, I don't know whether God would call me Marty or Martha. In fact, at the moment I don't like either name. I feel rather nameless."

Praying further in this direction was certainly blocked, so we paused, and I asked Marty if she could tell us what was her first hurtful memory.

"My first hurtful memory," she responded, "has already been healed through prayer. But the second one hasn't. When I was a little tot my mother got me dressed up in my finest clothes so we could visit my father at his job. We caught the bus, all excited to go on the adventure. When we arrived, though, he met us at the office door and told us to go home, and closed the door on us." Marty looked down at the bare floor and said, "It was a deep rejection to both of us then, and I guess it's a deep rejection in my memories now, since I haven't been able to deal with it."

I knew this would need to be prayed about but now wasn't the right time. We needed to begin with an easier memory. I felt Jesus wanted to bring integration between Marty's adult-self and her inner child. We asked the Holy Spirit to lead us. Marty saw herself in a pastoral setting, and thought she saw Jesus there, but then knew it wasn't He since she felt afraid. We cast out any evil influence. Scripture says God's Word is like a two-edged sword, able to distinguish between spirit and soul, so we took this "sword of the Spirit" and separated the true picture of Jesus and the picture of her earthly father (Hebrews 4:12). Since children often see God as they see their father, one can get superimposed over the other.

Marty had told us earlier her father and mother, though hard-working middle-class folks, developed serious problems with alcohol, which became apparent when she was around twelve. She knew her father had molested her in her childhood but she had repressed the memory of it. All she could remember was that she was constantly on the run as he pursued her, especially on the weekends, when both parents were drunk. She obviously had a frightening "picture" of "father."[5]

The next thing Marty could see was Jesus in a green meadow but couldn't see herself there with Him. Pat asked, "Can you see yourself there as a little lamb?"

Psalm 23—The Key

That was the key. Marty said she was able to experience herself being there as a little lamb, and felt safe with Jesus even though He was a Man. She ran up and sat on His lap and then ran away again. She could come and go as she pleased. No one was trying to control her. They frolicked together. I began quoting Psalm 23—personalizing it. Marty saw herself with Jesus "resting in green pastures," "walking beside still waters," as He "restored her soul" and led her in "paths of righteousness." She had a wonderful time, and we all rejoiced in her freedom. This was important because she told us that as a child she had always felt trapped because of her father's pursuit.

When the prayer session was completed and we were making plans for another, Marty said she felt guilty taking our time. We said we were delighted to be with her; it was our joy. She began to sob and sob. We put our arms around her and let her release grief and sorrow until she came to rest in God's unconditional love.

We're learning more about the children of alcoholic parents today.[6] So often the child had to become the parent while the parent became the child; the child has to give so much that it's hard for him or her to be in a position to receive. Marty was now receiving some of the love and caring that she had needed and deserved so many years before.

Marty, Pat, and I went our separate ways until the next afternoon. Back at my room I wrote some notes about the session and ideas for future prayers.

A few days following the Conference, Marty wrote me her account of our prayer time, telling the story from her perspective:

A Letter From Marty

Dear Rita,

If nothing else had happened, if I'd totally blocked . . . and fought the prayers, the fact that you spent so much time with me was deeply healing. For me, time is love. And you and Pat were both very loving.

I get nervous when too much time passes and I'm doing all the talking. You remember the first session we had, and I admitted how guilty I felt about taking up too much of your time? I was terrified of being rejected because I was so needy. But you didn't seem concerned about that. When you and Pat hugged me all I could do was cry.

Your working with me that first session helped me realize that I am acceptable just the way I am. I didn't have to be someone special in order to be healed. It was okay just to relax and be receptive. I think visualizing myself as a little lamb in Jesus' care was helpful because it did circumvent a lot of my feelings about father-daughter relationships. Seeing myself as a little lamb was easier than seeing myself as a little girl.

The other significant thing that happened during that first session was my realization that rejecting my given name, not wanting to hear Jesus call me by that name during the prenatal prayer, implied more than just not liking the name "Martha." It was rejection of part of myself, and I guess a rejection of those who named me. But for me to reject what my parents had called me, and to want to name myself, was like disconnecting myself from my source of life. I need to accept all my connections, especially those to my family, no matter how difficult or painful they are. Running away doesn't help. Jesus may have to redeem the relationships; He may have to remodel them so that they transmit life rather than suffering, but He doesn't seem willing to ignore them.

Thoughts From My Notebook

In my steno notebook I wrote:

Marty said she saw herself as neither male nor female in her picture of herself as a lamb. In future prayers she will need to see herself in a feminine role, able to receive healthy love from Jesus and other masculine figures, especially her father. Conflict: Needed father's love but couldn't receive it as he offered her the wrong kind of love. Today she doesn't know how to rest or play as a result of this pattern. Needs to forgive her father on different emotional levels, in different memories; needs to be healed and forgive in the second hurtful conscious memory when rejected at her father's office. As the Holy Spirit brings it to her conscious memory, incest experience(s) must be healed. Needs to see father as he could have been if he had been a whole person. Needs her father's affirmation.

Marty also needs help receiving her mother's love. Had a difficult birth with umbilical cord around her neck, and was born blue; had a fast birth but it was a breech birth. When she was born it was a national holiday; the doctor was busy with his family dinner and was late; this brought feelings of rejection. She needs to forgive the doctor. The unhappy first weeks of her life were due in part to Marty's mother trying to breast-feed her with nutritionally deficient milk, and it was several months before the problem was discovered. At some point Marty needs to finish prenatal prayer and receive Jesus' love and her mother's love.

She needs to forgive her mother for not protecting her from her father's advances. The mother was usually drunk on weekends, and each time her daughter approached her for help, she would roll over on the bed and pass out.

Each day at the Conference, we met new people, a very interesting and talented group: artists, writers, dancers, musicians, singers, and actors, as well as teachers, counselors, accountants, and other business people. One attractive, masculine young man, who happened to be from my own hometown in Florida, gave me a tape of his testimony on how through prayer he had been delivered from life as a "drag queen."

Most of the conferees were young people who are leaders in Exodus ministries from all over North America and few from other countries. They were so open and transparent about their lives it was most refreshing. Many were there seeking further healing. A small number were parents looking for answers for their children, and there were some ministers needing help for people in their congregations.

Prayer Two

The next day, Thursday, I was eager to see what the Lord would do for Marty. It was the Fourth of July but I didn't know God would have some special fireworks of His own ready!

All the afternoon workshops and evening meetings had been canceled for the holiday. Dennis and I were to meet at noon with Norman and Eleanor Smaha, my brother-in-law and sister-in-law by marriage, to spend the afternoon and evening together.

I caught the elevator to Marty's floor and walked down the empty hallway to her room. She was waiting and soon Pat joined us. We hugged one another and sat down.

Marty looked happy and eager to begin. We discussed some of the workshops and decided we had heard some of the best teachings available on healing, and restoration of femininity and masculinity.

The three of us reviewed what the Lord had done the previous day. I shared some of my notes to give direction for our prayer together.

There was identity confusion:

1. Marty's father had wanted a boy.

2. To be Martha was to be sexually pursued by her father.

3. She had repressed her femininity and preferred the masculine name, Marty (I found that her mother had done the same thing with her name—changing it from feminine to masculine).[7]

   4. Marty sometimes felt like a nonperson and during the first
      prayer session didn't want to be called by either name.

Integration Between Child and Adult

It seemed obvious that the next step was to pray for reconciliation between adult and child. Pat asked the Lord to help Marty
sense the support of His Presence, and that all we said and did
would be under His protection. After we prayed silently for a few
moments I said, "Marty, God wants to call you forth into life.
When you are aware of Jesus' Presence I'd like you, the adult
Marty, to say to the child Martha, 'Little Martha, I allow you to
live.' " We waited in quiet . . .

Marty tried to say the words, "Little Ma-Mar-Marth—oh, I just
can't!"

I asked, "Would you like me to say the words first and you follow?"

"That would help."

I began, "Little Martha . . ."

Marty repeated the words of reconciliation slowly with sobs,
"Little Mar-Martha . . ."

I went on, "I allow you to live."

Gasping out the words she cried, "I . . . oh . . . I allow you . . . to
live!" She fell over my lap, sobbing and gasping for breath. After
some time passed she cried, "She's been buried alive!" More sobs.
Pat and I reached out in loving support.

Several minutes later Marty went on talking to little Martha in
her own words, "I've been afraid to see you and accept you because
. . . I can't accept being needy. It's *not* okay for me to be needy and
dependent and to need nurturing. But I allow you, little Martha, to
be needy and to be nurtured by me and others. And through that, I
allow you to grow up."[8]

Marty then told us she was seeing big Marty pick up little
Martha and hold her. Then she saw her put her on her shoulders

and carry her piggyback style. She was getting reacquainted with her inner child.

A while later I ventured, "Now let's have the restored little Martha forgive big Marty. You can follow me again if you like:

"Big Marty . . ."

She repeated, "Big Marty. . . ."

"I forgive you . . ."

"I for . . . forgive you." As she tried to go on, tears flowed again. I waited.

When she was ready, she spoke forgiveness; again we started together, and she went on to finish by herself.

Seeing herself as little Martha she said, "Big Marty, I forgive you for not letting me live. I have hated you. But I forgive you. I choose to love you and accept you."

With tears running down her face, Marty cried out, "I've been resurrected!"

Resurrection on the Fourth of July

We praised the Lord, hugged one another, and praised some more. The fireworks were exploding in pinks, reds, blues, and yellows. Fourth of July celebration began early that day!

It was close to noon, and realizing my family would be waiting, I briefly discussed plans for our third and final prayer time. As we got up to leave, Marty remained seated on the hide-a-bed and said, "I'm exhausted; now I know how Jairus's daughter probably felt after coming back from the dead! I need to lie down and rest for a while."

I thought the comparison with Jairus's daughter was a good one. When Jesus raised her from the dead, the first thing He did was ask that she be given something to eat. But when Martha came back from psychological death, instead of food she needed sleep!

Pat and I prayed for the Holy Spirit to seal the work, said our good-byes, and quietly left the room. But fireworks were still going

off in our hearts, and we were nearly walking on air. You see, we'd
never been to a resurrection before!

The Second Session (Marty's View)

Here's what Marty said in a letter to me regarding our second
prayer session together:

The second session we had together involved reconciling me to myself, getting Big Marty to accept Little Martha, and helping Little
Martha to forgive Big Marty for rejecting her. You started with the
Adult Me first, having me envision myself talking to the Little Child
within me, which I've always rejected—the part of me which has needs,
which is dependent on others. You led me in an apology to the child
within me, which I was able to repeat after you but it took concentra-
tion and some effort. The child I once was had been so completely rejected that it felt buried alive and forgotten. My sobbing was also due to
my recognition that I'd been raised from the dead—that the part of me
which I had refused to allow expression was not only tolerated but respected. I had actually been the one to bury myself. My parents had
provided the model for my doing it, but I'd done this terrible thing to
myself.

Then you had me speak as Little Martha to Big Marty, forgiving the
Adult Me (the rational, competent, work-oriented aspect of myself) for
having rejected the dependent part of me which is helpless to meet her
own needs. As you cued me to say to my adult-self, "I forgive you . . ." I
broke down and wept again. The child that is still within me was able to
express her anger, and even her hatred, toward the repressive part of me.
And even as I did it, I realized that I was speaking simultaneously to
myself and my mother. The two realities were superimposed on each
other. And I knew I had internalized the external reality of my childhood (or at least my perception of it).

What was done to me, I have also done to myself. And I have to
admit, I do it to other people too. I am amazed at the similarities between outer circumstances and inner, between parents and children, between the family and more remote relationships. Repetition seems to be

everywhere. But now I know that Jesus can save us. He can stop this compulsion to repeat.

Prayer Three

There was a bittersweet feeling about our final prayer session. What we had experienced together in the Lord would always give us a closeness though we live in widely diverse parts of the USA.

It is important to have a good beginning before going on to more hurtful times. Those first sessions had prepared us for praying about Marty's second most hurtful memory. We agreed she was now ready for some basic healing with her father. But let her tell you about how the Holy Spirit led her in creative prayer. (In creative prayer, Jesus, our ever-present Lord, shows us what He, if allowed, would have done in our lives to help us, and actually lets us experience now with Him in our emotions. He doesn't change history but changes the history of the heart. The proof of the Holy Spirit's work is in the healings that occur.)

Marty's Version of the Third Session

In the third session, an old memory of rejection when I was a child was healed. In my imagination, as we prayed the Lord took me step-by-step through my proud mother's getting me—her first baby—dressed up and taking me on the bus to my father's office to show me off to his co-workers. My father met her at the door and told her he didn't have time for us, and I watched him shut the door in our faces. I sensed my mother's hurt and bewilderment, then her anger at me as we silently rode back home on the bus.

I felt confusion about what I'd done wrong that she was mad at me. She had put me down abruptly in my crib and gone into the other room of the apartment to be by herself. Then I saw Jesus come over to the crib and pick me up. Carrying me in His arms, He walked over to the window and looked out for a long time until He saw my father coming home from work.

Jesus sat down in the overstuffed chair next to the crib and continued to hold me, as my father came into the apartment and into the bedroom. My dad was surprised to see Jesus holding me, and didn't quite know what to do. My dad told Jesus that I was his daughter. Jesus looked him right in the face and said, "I know." But Jesus didn't move or say anything more.

Then my father began pacing around the room, frustrated and confused. At one point he slammed his fist against the wall. I know he didn't know how to be a father, because his own dad had left his wife and children to try to find work during the depression and had suffered a mental breakdown from which he never recovered.

But then Jesus quietly asked my father, "Do you want your daughter?"

And my dad said, "Yes."

So Jesus got up from the chair to let my father sit down; and Jesus put me into his arms. Uncertain, my father started to give me back to Jesus, but Jesus encouraged him to keep me.

. . . My mother looked at my father and told him how hurt she was that he had shut us out as if we weren't important. My father looked back at her and exclaimed, "I can't afford to socialize at work. I could lose my job! I don't have the education to do what they want me to do, and it's taking me more time than anyone else to do the work."

I know if my dad had lost his job, he would have had a very hard time finding another one. Because of my grandfather's breakdown, my father had completed only the ninth grade, and in 1947 that wasn't much to compete against all the other returning soldiers who also needed work. And I realized that working to support us was the only way my dad knew how to be a father. My mother must've realized it too, because she bent down, gently took his hand, and kissed his fingers. Then she touched his face and said quietly. "I'm sorry." My father looked down at me, then back at her and asked, "What's for supper?" and all the tension was gone.

After the third session, I was so weak I could hardly stand up. I also felt some nausea, like my insides had been rearranged. I had to lie down for about half an hour to let the impact of that session settle. I still don't know how inner healing happens, but it's certainly not a superficial experience. If I said "thank you" a thousand times, it wouldn't be enough.

P.S. Rita, I don't know if it's your usual style or whether the Lord led you especially to do it with me, but I was deeply comforted by your freedom to hug me. For a long time (maybe always) I've felt unclean, like a person with a contagious disease that no one dare touch. . . . I think I know how the lepers felt when Jesus touched them. Thank you for not being afraid of me. I wish I could tell you, but it's deeper than any words.

Before Dennis and I left to return to Seattle, Marty told me happily that Pat had invited her to spend a few days with her and her husband, who lived nearby. This was a good follow-up to our three-day prayer session. I also encouraged Marty to meet with our mutual friend, Barb, and her prayer partner, when she got back home. I knew she would need more prayer in areas we hadn't had time to cover and those not yet revealed. For example, the Holy Spirit hadn't brought up any memories of incest, so obviously that would need to be dealt with later.

Over the summer months I thought of and prayed for Marty and wondered how she was doing. I wrote to her. On September 1, I heard from her again:

Marty Writes After the Conference

Dear Rita,

I was delighted to get your letter the other day! I still haven't gotten over the impact of our time together, partly because the Lord keeps building on it day by day. One of the reasons for this letter—besides just to touch base with you—is to let you know what's been going on since Exodus.

This has been a really unusual summer for me. I've never had a period of my life like it. In a way I feel like I've been out in the desert with Jesus or John the Baptist—and in another way, it's felt like I've been lying on the surgeon's table for three months (you are one of the surgeons). It's been glorious and awful, alternating between periods of peace and agony. Many times I've wanted to run away (although there's nowhere to run to), but sometimes I've felt the Lord closer than breathing. In a way, I'm almost sorry that it will soon be over, since I start back teaching on September 9, but then I remember that the Lord knows what He's doing. I either need a breather or He'll be working on me in some different way when school is in session.

Anyway, to let you know what's been happening . . . I couldn't get an inner-healing session with Barb and Anne until a couple of weeks ago, since one or the other of them was out of town the whole month of July and the first part of August. But while I was waiting, the Lord was working on me Himself. I've been seeing a counselor (a Catholic nun) for a couple of years now, and I told her about my experiences with you and Pat in San Francisco. She encouraged me to put myself in the Lord's Presence and try to work through the relationship between the Adult Me and the Little Child within.

So for several days in the late afternoon I got quiet before the Lord and let that theme develop. For three evenings the scenes came without any trouble. The main theme that evolved over this time was: the anger of the Little Child (actually she was about twelve) because of my father's molestations, and the fear of being trapped in my house with no way of escape.

A week later, after another session with my counselor, I had a couple of evenings of meditation again by myself. In one I realized the terrific ambivalence the Little Child inside me feels about the Adult Me—alternating between defiant rage and desperate clinging. The other opened up for me some of the meaning behind the breast-feeding motif, which keeps popping up.

In one of the scenes I am aware of how starved the Little Child is, and how she pulls and pulls the milk out of me in long, desperate draughts. Then I remember that my mother told me she had tried to breast-feed me when I was born and didn't know for a couple of months that her milk was inadequate. But when she put me on a bottle, she carefully followed the doctor's orders to feed me only every four hours (this was in the 1940s), so I continued to be half-starved.

What I apparently did as an infant was say to myself, "If I can't have it, then I don't need it," because I grew up as a skinny little kid who ate almost nothing. I guess I learned, if you don't expect much you won't feel rejected.

One thing that I noticed a couple of weeks ago, rather spontaneously, was that *my lifelong skin hunger—the excessive need to be hugged, held, touched—that need is pretty much gone.* When I slept with people I used to want to be in contact with them in some way—if they were willing, I'd wrap myself around them koala-bear-style, but the desperate hunger for physical contact now seems to be satisfied. *I consider that no small miracle.* I still like normal contact, but the intense drive is gone.

Prayer-Counseling at Home

The next section of Marty's letter tells of several meetings with her prayer-counselors at home.

On the 22 and 23 of August I had inner-healing sessions with Barb and Anne. On the first day we mostly talked about my life (which Anne knew little of, though Barb had heard it before). I wasn't sure what we needed to deal with—my anger toward a man currently in my life, my attitude toward my mother's (current) drinking, or my dislike of my name.

Anne started out by asking me what name I wanted. I said, "Katherine" like Katharine Hepburn or Catherine Marshall (both strong, respectable women, from my point of view, not wimps or lost souls totally dominated by men). We realized what a lousy view of women I have and how I need to see women from Jesus' point of view. So Barb took the sword of the Spirit and cut me free from my old conception of what it means to be a woman (passive, used, nonperson), and Anne prayed that I would see myself through Jesus' eyes, as the woman God designed.

One other topic that got covered in the first session was that Anne challenged me on my claim that I'd never been rebellious. She said that rebellion is central to our sin-nature. So between the first and second session I asked the Lord to show me how I'd been rebellious. What came up was that rebellion can take two forms. The one I'd been less guilty of was doing what people tell you not to do: deliberate defiance of authority. But I was guilty of not doing what I was expected to do: sin of omission. Inner vows like, "I'll never be like my mother!"—these are rebellious statements and they needed to be given up and broken.

Breaking Inner Vows

So in the second session [with Barb and Anne] I confessed them and asked that the vows be broken. I also recognized that something like a spirit of fear (with regard to men, especially) utterly controlled me. I wanted it gone. I also wanted all the bonds with everyone I'd ever slept with broken. I wanted to clean up my sexuality on every level. I can't remember which we did first, the deliverance or the breaking of the bonds.

In the deliverance prayer we went prenatally all the way back to conception, and I suddenly realized that the stiffness in me, the fear of men, might have been in my mother in the act of intercourse which led to my conception. . . . Perhaps I had been conceived in fear, although my mother had very much wanted a baby. That's the reason I felt the fear in my very bones, in my every cell. So Anne commanded the spirit of fear to leave my body, my bones, my cells. And I realized that part of me wanted to hang onto that fear because it was my only defense against abuse. So we stopped the deliverance prayer until I told Jesus that I wanted Him as my Defense and not any attitude of my own.

Then I realized that I couldn't be free of the fear until I prayed for my mother to be free; we were connected spiritually somehow, and I couldn't stand leaving her in her fear while I left mine behind. So I asked Jesus to release my mother from her fear (which is more pervasive than mine, I think. It affects all her relationships, not just those with men). Then we could proceed with deliverance prayer, which was rather quiet and peaceful.

In breaking the inner vows, I recognized two specifically that needed to be given up. One was, of course, "I'll never be like my mother," which certainly bound me to be exactly like her—if not in form, certainly in spirit. The other was a vow I made when I was a senior in high school and the boy who'd asked me to the prom backed out on the morning of the dance. I have no recollection of the event at all, but my mother said that I put down the telephone receiver and declared, "I'll never let any boy do that to me again."

I had had two or three significant dreams between the first and second inner-healing sessions, one of which had Jesus in it—not as the historically pictured Jesus but like a modern man. In breaking the vows, I imagined this (modern) Jesus lifting His foot to stamp down on a stiff piece of lumber, breaking it in half. . . . Then suddenly I realized that not only was the board my vow, but it was me—that my fear had made me stiff and rigid as a board, and that I had'gotten just that way every time my father approached me for affection. I had in my fear of him reacted just like my mother, by getting stiff and unresponsive, absolutely terrified.

He had molested me, so there was legitimate cause for my fear, but part of it appeared to have been passed down from my mother. So when He broke the vow, He broke it inside of me, and I literally fell forward into Barb's arms and sobbed out the emotional stiffness toward men that had always been in me.

At this point, Barb wanted to take the sword of the Spirit and cut me free from each person I had ever slept with. One by one I named them, male and female, and asked forgiveness for what I'd done. As I mentioned each relationship, Barb said, "I take the sword of the Spirit and sever all your emotional and spiritual ties with [person's name], and I seal the ends with the blood of Jesus, so they can never be rejoined. I ask the Lord to set you completely free from any one-flesh relationship with that person." (I had decided before the session that I wanted this severing to happen, but hadn't mentioned it to either Anne or Barb. But the Spirit of the Lord knew.)

After all this was over, I felt as limp as a dishrag. We all felt that was everything we needed to do for now. What still remained was for me to deliberately choose to renew my mind with regard to my own function in life, my relationship to men, my vision of femininity and so on. I've opened myself up for Jesus to bring whatever I need into my life.

A Healing Side Effect

Marty's letter continued:

One side effect of these inner-healing sessions was that my attitude toward my relatives immediately and dramatically changed. I have two first cousins living in the same city as I do, whom I haven't seen or talked to in years, and I've always dodged contact with my aunts and uncles. Suddenly, I wanted contact with them, and even arranged to eat lunch with an elderly aunt of mine who was so astonished with it that she called her brother living in another state to tell him about it!

This opening up to my family was totally unexpected but is going to make a lot of difference in my attitude about feeling isolated. Part of my detachment I learned from my mother, but it is my responsibility from this point on. Forgiving and praying for my mother and breaking those vows (and the deliverance prayer) has set me free in ways I never expected.

When more things develop, I'll let you know about them. I can't tell you how much I appreciate and cherish you. Blessings be upon you and Dennis. May our Lord dump a big load of joy and His glory upon your heads!

In January 1986 I received Marty's okay to use her story in this book. In her letter two things stand out that I want to quote for you,

What has happened since the September letter is that I've realized how deeply rooted my problem with men is and how I need continued help to move through it, so I'll be going to a therapy group for adult survivors of incest beginning in February. I think this is the next, essential step in my healing.

Almost all of my sexual attraction toward women is gone.

Healing continues with Marty in the same way it can with any of us. Like the layers of an onion, the Lord removes one layer of wounds to get to another. The healing of an identity problem may take several years (two to four, and sometimes more) of consistent prayer ministry—depending, of course, on how deep the need is.

I received a written testimony from Carrie Wingfield, who was completely healed from homosexuality after four years of soul-healing prayer. In a letter to me she explains:

I believe it is possible for God to completely free us from homosexual struggles over a period of time, as He does a healing in our hearts of all the bitterness, rage, and anger talked about in Ephesians 4. It definitely is a process, and we cannot put a time limit on it; but I do believe that total healing and release from homosexual struggles and attractions is possible.

Carrie's wounds came from sources similar to and different from Marty's. She is now praying for others under the supervision of her church, Saint Luke's Episcopal, in Seattle. She says she is thankful even for the homosexual pain she went through, now that it's bearing fruit for God.

Many different people may be involved in a person's healing. There were many who worked with Marty, as you can see from her letters. There were psychological counselors and inner-healing prayer-counselors. Her receiving Jesus into her life and the release of the Holy Spirit were two major inner-healing experiences which made all the rest possible. Now she is in a support group for women with similar needs, which will help her discover more things she can take to Jesus in prayer. Psychology, even Christian psychology, may be helpful for diagnosis but without prayer to follow it up, it's limited in making in-depth changes in a person's life.

Marty's already passing on what she's received. Marty made and is making peace with Martha; she's making peace with her parents, with her relatives, with the men and women in her life. And the world will feel it. It will be a better place because of one tiny, vivacious woman called Marty.

In the next chapter we'll talk about how you can receive inner peace. . . .

Soul-Healing Prayers

Breaking Wrong Inner Vows Prayer.[9] If you are still carrying the effect of wrong inner vows made against your mother/father, you need to make them powerless over your life. Have you made vows like these, "*I will never:* be like my mother (or father) [this sets you up to *be* like her or him!] . . . love and forgive my mother/father for what was done; . . . acknowledge him/her as my parent; . . . see my parent again; . . . give him/her the satisfaction of my public affirmation; or . . ." [fill in others here].

Pray in this way: "I choose to give up these rebellious vows and I ask You to break them, Lord. Please remove any negative effects from my life.

Any wrong spirit that has oppressed me as a result of these vows, I renounce you and command you to leave and have no further influence over me, in Jesus' name; and through His cleansing blood I pray.

Lord, please fill me now with Your Holy Spirit. Thank You, Lord Jesus. Amen."

Prayer for Breaking Wrong Sexual Ties. I've found that people's souls can be knit together for blessing or bondage. Someone who has had a premarital or extramarital heterosexual love affair, or a homosexual love affair, may still be psychologically tied to the person with whom he had the affair. Such a tie must be broken.

After asking your heavenly Father to forgive you and claiming John 1:9 for your cleansing, pray the following prayer:

"Father God, in the name of Jesus, I acknowledge a wrong soul tie between myself and _____. Scripture says the yoke [tie between us] will be broken because of God's anointing [Isaiah 10:27]; and God's anointing abides in His people [1 John 2:27]. I take this sword of the Spirit and cut myself free from all wrong soul ties of intellect, will, and emotions. I ask You, Father, to set me completely free from any one-flesh relationship with him [or her]. I seal the prayer with the blood of Jesus. In Jesus' name I pray."

Claim the promise of Galatians 5:1, "When Christ freed us, he meant us to remain free. Stand firm, therefore, and do not submit again to the yoke of slavery" (JERUSALEM).

(Please note here I am not talking of having a soul tie to someone who has departed this life. Such a tie would be broken at death, although its influence might remain in memory, and need to be forgiven and healed.)

Chapter Three

A Gift
of Peace
for You

"Peace I leave with you,
My peace I give unto you. . . .
Let not your heart be troubled,
neither let it be afraid."

John 14:27
The words of Jesus Christ

True healing of your soul is *only* possible through Jesus Christ, His death, and His Resurrection. The Hebrew word for peace, *shalom,* speaks of the wholeness and integration of one's entire being. In the Septuagint Greek Version of the Scriptures, *shalom* is often translated *soteria,* which means: salvation, preservation, health, and deliverance.

Peace within comes from two directions:

1. Identifying with Christ in His "earth walk."

2. Letting the resurrected Lord walk with you through the still-unhealed wounds of your past, and then walk with you to heal you day by day.

Isaiah 53 is the most complete prophetic description of Jesus Christ in the Old Testament. Look at it and see how you can identify with Jesus (vv. 2–5 JERUSALEM):

> *Like a sapling he grew up in front of us,*
> *Like a root in arid ground.*
> *Without beauty, without majesty (we saw him),*
> *no looks to attract our eyes;*
> *a thing despised and rejected by men,*
> *a man of sorrows and familiar with suffering,*
> *a man to make people screen their faces;*
> *he was despised and we took no account of him.*
>
> *And yet ours were the sufferings he bore,*
> *ours the sorrows he carried.*
> *But we, we thought of him as someone punished,*
> *struck by God, and brought low.*
> *Yet he was pierced through for our faults,*
> *crushed for our sins.*
> *On him lies a punishment that brings us peace,*
> *and through his wounds we are healed.*

This picture of Jesus Christ shows that He had hurts (although *He* was without sin). You can identify with Him, and as you do, you can also identify with His family:

He was carried in a mother's womb, as you were.

His foster father, Joseph, considered divorce before Jesus was born as he did not understand Jesus' supernatural conception.

Mary experienced a long and tiring ride on that little donkey, just before giving birth to Jesus, possibly experiencing labor pains near the end of the journey. The unborn Jesus would have shared in the discomfort.

He may have sensed the rejection his parents felt when there wasn't a proper place for them to rest, nor for Him to be born. So He was rejected even before He was born.

Did you ever wonder who delivered Baby Jesus? Don't you suppose it must have been His foster father, Joseph? But Psalms 22:9, 10 also tells us that God the Father assisted at His Son's birth. The omnipresent God was there when you were born too.

Though He was the King, He wasn't born in a palace, but in a stable with straw for His bed. In one way this was one of the most beautiful places to be born, surrounded by the loving animals He had created, but it was neither comfortable, convenient, nor sanitary.

When He took His first breath, it hurt just as it did with you. He felt the change from the buoyancy of amniotic fluid to the gravitational pull of the earth.

Jesus was bonded to His foster father, Joseph, and His mother, Mary, as they looked into His eyes those first minutes after birth. You can be bonded to Him as by faith you see Him as He looked into your eyes at *your* birth.

Baby Jesus learned to walk, just as you did. Think how happy Joseph and Mary were when He took His first step! The most important step ever taken on the earth was when Jesus took His first baby step and from there began the process of claiming back this world for God's kingdom.

He experienced His parents' fears when Herod the King ordered all children two years old and under to be killed, and He and His parents had to escape to Egypt.

Jesus was a gifted Child and perhaps found it difficult to be understood by His peers. On a journey with His parents, they suddenly discovered that He was missing and after much effort found Him in the Temple conversing with the doctors and the lawyers. Even then they didn't understand (Luke 2:48).

He worked in the family business. Who knows what kind of challenges there were, working with the public and getting along with His family?

At the age of thirty, Jesus began to proclaim the good news of the kingdom and to do miracles. From then, to the end of His earthly life, hurt and rejection escalated until the Cross.

Questions for You

Were you rejected by your family, race, or religious group? Jesus was "despised and rejected of men" (Isaiah 53:3).

Do people, including your family, not understand your ministry? It was the same with Him (Mark 3:21–25).

Do people disapprove of those who are your friends? It was the same with Jesus (Matthew 9:11).

Have you been accused of being of the devil? So was Jesus (Luke 11:15, 18).

Did your father die, leaving you to care for your mother and family? Jesus' foster father died before Jesus began His ministry, and as the oldest son, He would have had to take the responsibility of caring for His mother and family.

Were you betrayed by a close friend? So was He (Matthew 26:48, 49).

Did you lose one of your best friends in death? So did He (John 11:25, 36).

Were you beaten, spit upon, eyes blackened shut? He was too (Matthew 27:26–30).

Did all your friends but a very few leave you at the time of your worst trial? Jesus had the same experience (Matthew 26:56).

You may say "but Jesus didn't have an alcoholic father as I had"; "He wasn't molested as I was"; or "He didn't have a learning disability as I have." That's true; but because He is with you and loves you, He suffers when you suffer . . . He experiences your pain along with you. Just as you hurt when your children are hurting, so it is with Jesus and you.

> *Jesus came to earth to identify with you,*
> *so that you in response could identify with Him.*

The Example of David

David, a young man in his late teens, is an example of someone who identified with Jesus in healing prayer. One of the unhappy memories David had as a child of four or five was the sound of his father using the belt on his rebellious older brother. David would lie in bed and hear the frightening yells and angry words. Because the older brother also beat up on his little brother, sometimes David would "tell on" his big brother, but this made him feel responsible for his brother's punishment.

Whether this was real guilt or imposed guilt, it seemed that David needed to ask Jesus to forgive him if in any way he had been wrong. As we prayed, I let God's Word speak forgiveness to him by quoting the Scripture, "If we confess our sins, He is faithful and just to forgive us our sins and to cleanse us from all unrighteousness" (1 John 1:9). I reminded David that when we repent we are completely free from sin and guilt.[1]

When David experienced the presence of Jesus in his room, comforting him as a child, he felt free to cry and let his hurts out. A little while later David saw Jesus going into his brother's room and taking the beating for him. He could even see the stripes on Jesus' back instead of his brother's back. Then David again saw himself in his own room in bed, and happily realized the frightening yells and angry words had ceased. He was at peace.

Since his brother didn't accept him in his childhood years, David discovered he also didn't like or accept his child-self. He spoke acceptance to his inner child through Jesus.

The passage in Isaiah 53:5 we previously looked at says, ". . . by His stripes we *are* healed" and 1 Peter 2:24 looking back to Calvary says, "by whose stripes you *were* healed" (italics added). *Here you have healing promised for your present and your past.* Still you have to enter into healing on each level, spirit, soul, and body in order to make it yours. David began doing that and step-by-step he is being healed in his soul.

A Gift for You

Most parents try to do the best they know how, but all of us make mistakes, some big ones, some little ones. When the world fell from God's original plan, the plan for an ideal family fell too. If your family chose to walk with God, you are fortunate, but God can't force people to choose Him and His ways. Even members of families who are in Christ can seriously hurt one another.

With Jesus it had to be different. He came into the world on a rescue mission. This mission had far more planning than was needed for sending a man to the moon. It took centuries to prepare a race of people for His coming, and then finally to locate the right couple to be His earthly parents. He couldn't be born into a family at random. His parents had to be able to listen to God, and willing to obey without question, so they could protect Jesus from destruction during His vulnerable childhood.

Joseph and Mary were the finest couple God could find to love and care for His own Son. The Scripture doesn't tell us much about them, but being chosen by God the Father is the best possible recommendation! The outstanding qualities we learn about them in the Gospel records are: *they obeyed God,* even if it meant loss of reputation, or death; *they kept the ordinances of their religion; they were faithful,* moving when God said move, regardless of inconvenience or danger; *they were spiritually sensitive,* being warned in dreams, having visions of angels, and respect for the supernatural gifts of the Spirit, as when prophecies were spoken over the Baby Jesus in the Temple. (*See* Matthew and Luke, chapters 1, 2 in both books.)

But the second reason God worked so hard at choosing this family was that *He chose them for you.* He wanted you to look at them and their example and to model after them! No, God couldn't make every family obedient to His will, but the Father gave you His Son and His Son's family to look up to.

> *Jesus' parents give you a picture*
> *of what God wanted your parents to be like.*

Whether you had a good set of parents or not, or whether you knew your parents at all, you can look to Joseph and Mary as your model parents.

Identifying with Christ is the undergirding basis for working through damaged emotions and memories. By His stripes you were healed. Enter into this promise: You will also receive the gift of peace as you allow the resurrected Lord to walk with you into those still-unhealed places.

Some of you will need to make peace with your *inner* parents . . .

Reflection

Think of how you can identify with Jesus in His walk on Earth. In what way is your life the same as His? In what way are your hurts in life different from His? How were your parents different from Jesus' earthly parents? (*Pause and if you wish write your answers.*)   Think of how Joseph and Mary, or some other surrogate parents you admire, would have handled a situation that concerns you. Take time to thank God for wholesome parents and/or model parents. (*Pause.*)

Chapter Four

Making Peace
With Your
Inner Parents

*It's the value God places upon you
that's important,
not what your parents think about you
or anyone else.*

Author unknown

This is not a chapter on "How to get along with your parents"; or "How to be a good parent," though people needing such help will benefit from it and the chapters following. There are many books on these topics written by others more experienced than I. There aren't many available, however, to tell you what to do *after* the fact. What do you do with past hurts that affect your life and relationship with your parents now? Or what can you do with the hurtful memories from parents who are no longer living? These are problems I want to help you with.

The most important relationships in your formative years (which still affect you now) are with your mother and father. To some people that's not a surprise; others may say, "How can that apply to me?" or "I never knew my mother," or "I hardly ever saw my father." Well, it can. We are still affected in some way, whether our relationship with our parents was active or inactive.

What actually *was* your relationship with your parents? Positive or negative? The following is a sampling of some people who were affected negatively by their relationships with their parents but later received soul restoration through prayer:

A former *"pornoholic"* said, "My parents divorced when I was three years old. I lost both of them as my father moved out and my mother went to work away from home."

A former *lesbian* said, "My mother and father were alcoholics, and my father pursued me sexually most of my teenage years."

A former *mental patient* said, "My mother and father were both professional people and neither one had time for me."

A former *emotionally retarded person* said, "My parents were divorced when I was thirteen, just when I needed my father's love so much. Losing him in this way made me feel rejected by him and caused a break in our relationship which lasted for years."

A former *"gay"* said, "I was tied to my mother's apron strings. My father totally rejected me and tried to kill me before my birth."

Undoubtedly there are other factors which, added to these early ones, caused those major problems. Yet the parental foundation and continuing influence of parents is awesome.

Have you ever heard Christians say something like this? "The parents you have are the ones God designed specifically for you. You should thank Him for having chosen them, since He knew exactly what you needed." This statement wouldn't bother someone who had the love of both parents and a happy childhood. But saying it to one with serious hurts and an unhappy childhood might cause them to question the very goodness of God!

We come back once again to the age-old question of the sovereignty of God. I don't intend to solve this in "one fell swoop," but I encourage you who are *not* wounded to be aware of the wounded around you. Realize, yes, God is ultimately sovereign in this universe, but has His total sovereignty "on hold" until His plan for the recovery of Planet Earth has been fulfilled, and He returns in Person to finish the job.

Meanwhile, God is counting on you and me, who have His sovereign kingdom in us, to do His healing work until Jesus returns. True, those of us who are in Christ can with joy say, "God is in charge of my life. Jesus reigns!" But before we accepted His Lordship, it was a different story. Even now, we are still in a battle between good and evil, and the warfare is not a game, but real.

I don't believe that during this Age of Grace God exercises the kind of control in which His perfect will is done in each life and every family on earth. I don't believe He's deciding from His throne, "I think I'll send this little baby to an alcoholic father who will try to destroy him, and I'll send this little baby girl to a father who will seduce her. These will be real learning experiences for them." No! Of course not! But all too often this is what Christians are unwittingly affirming.[1]

I've prayed with people who were afraid to consider their birth because of the horrors or sadness of the family they were born into. As we've prayed and relived their birth scenes with Jesus, they were only able to choose to accept their family *because Jesus guaranteed in His Word that His healing Presence would be with them.* Only then did they know everything would be okay, because they could allow Him to walk through those memories of the past and heal them day by day. They would be able to survive emotionally and mentally because they saw God's unconditional love for them.

God is standing by to make good out of any situation no matter how traumatic. As evidence to back up this statement, all of the preceding people (the former): pornoholic, lesbian, mental patient, emotionally retarded, and homosexual are now telling others what's happened to them, and many of them are praying for others to be healed in the same way. This is just a sampling of the truth I've seen repeated time and again, that as you release your hurts to God, no matter how damaging they may have been, He will turn them to good. It's even possible to say that God can make the outcome more beneficial to you and His kingdom than if the problem never occurred. Romans 8:28 is a Scripture you can trust your life to, "And we know that all things work together for good to those who love God, to those who are the called according to His purpose."

The Prejudiced Inner Parent

With Jesus and His family as a base on which to build, let's go ahead and see how you may be feeling about memories with your own parents. Within your child-self are the memories of your parents (or surrogate parents). The first five or six years were the most impressionable times in your life. Here motivations and judgments were implanted in you at an early age by those in authority over you. Your parents were godlike figures to your child-self. They had complete control over you. You felt, "Whatever they say or do must be right." What they said or did went into your child mind with no editing. It was law.

Parents aren't perfect, though some of you may have been blessed with parents who you felt were near to it. Some will have more need in this area than others; read on with that in mind. All parents have blind spots and prejudices, and though you may do your best not to, you carry with you some of the good and bad input from your parents, just as they did from theirs. That's why each person begins adult life with what I call a "prejudiced inner parent."

Your parents programmed your childhood attitudes for good or for ill. For example, negative concepts like these may have been imposed: "Never trust a minister; all politicians are crooked; everybody's out to get your money; all movies are bad; Indians, whites, blacks, orientals [you name it] are no good; our family is superior to others; people who smile too often must have something up their sleeves; she didn't go to the right school so don't get involved with her; discussing your sexuality is wrong; doctors just want your money; praising God with lifted hands is 'holy roller' stuff; my dad didn't like her so I won't like her either; he was raised on the wrong side of the tracks so don't get too friendly; don't get mixed up with a Protestant [or a Catholic]" and so forth. You may think of other imposed thought patterns.

A prejudiced parent may knowingly or unknowingly instill such preconceived judgments as these in the young child. They may be said to him directly, but often he takes them in by example, or from things his parents say to one another in his hearing. The little child has no way to evaluate whether these concepts are true or not; he absorbs the information "as is."

A friend of mine was taking care of a relative's son. He had been taught "movies are bad," and told his hostess emphatically that he wouldn't go to such places! Later she was surprised to find him sitting in front of the TV, watching a rather unsavory film. He didn't see any inconsistency in his behavior. His inner recordings said, "Movies are bad; TV is okay."[2] He hadn't been taught to evaluate, but only to obey blindly.

When you were a child, your parent's conscience, his or her beliefs of rights and wrongs, became your conscience. If he was very dogmatic and intense about what he felt you should believe, it may be hard for you to discover your own beliefs and become your own person; but with God's help you can lay aside the dictatorship of your inner parent. This does not mean you're rejecting your parent but are letting the impurities go and retaining the gold. The freedom God has for you will be limited if you continue to hold on to your prejudiced parent's influence.

Perhaps these are some of the "dead works" Scripture says our consciences need cleansing from, which was made possible by the sacrifice of Jesus. The writer of Hebrews states, "how much more effectively the blood of Christ, who offered himself as the perfect sacrifice to God through the eternal Spirit, can purify our inner self from dead actions so that we do our service to the living God" (Hebrews 9:14 JERUSALEM). And Paul said, "With this hope before me I do my utmost to live my whole life with a clear conscience before God and man" (Acts 24:16 PHILLIPS). You know, of course, that you need to repent of your sins, but how can you further cleanse and heal your soul?

Attaining Jesus' Perspective

Look through Jesus' eyes and perspective as you pray about memories in your childhood. Then you will be able to see your parents' beliefs objectively, their good and bad points, and you'll be able to choose what is good and let the rest go. The way to look at things through Jesus' eyes is to read and reread the Gospel records of what He was like, what He said, and what He did.

Most of the functions of your soul's intellect, will, and emotions are mixtures of right and wrong. As you let hurtful and prejudiced memories go, you will become more creative and mature, and may begin to love your parents for the first time, or to love them more than you have in the past.

It is not wrong to admit that you have a problem or hurt connected with a parent, and talking to someone about it doesn't dishonor the parent. If you dislike or even hate your parent, you honor them by talking to a *trustworthy* person about the problem, praying about it, getting the memory healed, and going on to genuinely love them. Even if your parent has died, it's never too late for you to be healed, and to forgive, and love him or her. It *is* wrong to talk about your hurts over and over again with people at random, never praying about your memories, and therefore not being healed. This is *gossip*, which ultimately helps no one, including you.

It is vitally important to pray inner-healing for yourself, or (if your needs are very deep) to have qualified prayer partners assist you.[3] This is one of the best ways to practice God's healing Presence in your life, allow Him to give you His perspective, and be cleansed from wrong parental commands in your soul.

To Obey Your Parents or Not to Obey?

God's commandment to children listed in the Old Testament is "Honour thy father and thy mother, as the Lord thy God hath commanded thee; that thy days may be prolonged, and that it may go well with thee, in the land which the Lord thy God giveth thee." (Deuteronomy 5:16 KJV; *see also* Exodus 20:12). Notice that the original command was simply to "honour". Paul adds to this command the idea of "obedience." "Children, obey your parents in the Lord . . ." (Ephesians 6:1-3). Then he immediately says, "And you, fathers, do not provoke your children to wrath, but bring them up in the training and admonition of the Lord" (Ephesians 6:4).

Teachers on family life have renewed the warning, and rightly so, on the importance of honoring our parents. "Things just don't go well" when we dishonor our parents. It's been said, "We expect results for disobeying physical laws but don't often think this way about spiritual laws. Many of the hurts we suffer are because of disobedience to spiritual laws."

Rebellion and disrespect to parents is ugly, and when you dishonor your parent, you really dishonor yourself. It has a boomerang effect. In our society we have too much of this behavior. We can learn something from oriental countries where there has been a tradition of respecting and taking care of parents, especially in old age.

Barbara McGowan, a very good friend of mine from high school and college days says, "The command to honor your parents applies to all parents whether they're biological or adoptive ones." She encourages adopted children to honor both sets of parents and says, "You can do this through prayer and in conversation about them. Often you will only be able to honor your biological parents when you can honor and love your adoptive parents." Barbara and her husband, Bill, have two beautiful adopted children now in their teens, George and Gina. Barbara says further, "I believe we must teach our children to honor all parents related to them for maximum wholeness: biological parents—ones God used to bring the child into this world; adoptive parents—ones chosen by God to take the child as their own to rear; stepparents—ones given by God for the continuing nurture of the child."

Honoring, Obeying, or Both?

But if parents aren't acting "in the Lord," or a father is "provoking children to wrath," is God really expecting the children to obey them in everything? Or we may ask, "Are we still honoring our parents if we feel we must disobey them in certain situations?" What if their command spoken or inferred is against God's will? For example, "You must have sex with me"; or "you must have nothing to do with races inferior to ours"; or "you must steal money to help me financially."

I remember visiting a dying mother in a hospital who shared with me in confidence that her husband had had incestuous relationships with their daughters over the years. She had shared this problem with her minister years before, but he offered no real help to the man or to the wife and children. All the guidance the girls heard at church in such matters was to "obey your parents"!

I've known some well-meaning Bible teachers to *paraphrase* the commandment from Ephesians to read something like, "Children obey your parents in the Lord, for this is right, *even if they are wrong!*" They feel that the child who obeys a wrong command, if given by their parents, will bask in God's approval.[4] I'm sure these teachers are referring to *normal* families when such ideas are taught, but what about children with emotionally *sick* parents?

In an excellent article called "The Incest Legacy," the author Diana Russell clearly shows that statistically there is a strong connection between childhood incest and later experiences of sexual assault. The child so treated develops various problems, such as: not trusting others, feeling powerless, lacking assertiveness to reject unwanted sexual advances, feeling isolated and guilty. Other results can take the form of extreme sexual frigidity, or on the other hand, may serve as a training ground for prostitution.[5]

I believe that while you're under your parents' roof and financially dependent on them, you should obey them in every way you possibly can. But if your parents break God's laws, He does not expect you to obey their wrong commands.

Of the Ten Commandments the one for children is fifth on the list, and is the first with an additional promise, one of longevity. However, the *very first* of the Ten Commandments is, "You shall have no other gods before Me" (Exodus 20:3). Jesus said that the first and greatest commandment in the law is "You shall love the Lord your God with all your heart, with all your soul, and with all your mind" (Matthew 22:37). When parents are breaking God's commands, there is a higher commandment, and that is of obeying and honoring God!

Your parents are not little gods! To make a human being a god is idolatry. When man's ways are contrary to God's clear instructions, you are never wrong to choose God's ways. (A young child may find it impossible to do anything about abuse until later, when the memories can then be healed through prayer.)

Looking to Jesus

You can always honor parents even though you can't always obey them. Jesus always honored His parents, yet He did not always obey them. At least once in His childhood Jesus made a decision without asking His parents. He stayed behind in Jerusalem to talk to the learned men in the Temple. Perhaps at twelve years of age He didn't realize the worry He would cause His family when He chose not to join the caravan on its return to Nazareth. However, after a three-day search, Joseph and Mary found Him, and He willingly honored them by returning home and submitting himself to them (Luke 2:41-52). Jesus bar-Joseph worked side by side with His foster father in the carpentry business for years. As I have noted, it seems Joseph must have died while Jesus was living at home. Jesus must have taken over the family business, until at the age of thirty He began His public ministry.

Jesus was so concerned about His mother's welfare that with His dying breath from the Cross He asked His good friend, John, to take her as his own mother (John 19:26, 27). Jesus always honored His earthly parents and, of course, His heavenly Father.

Yet again we know of a specific time in His adult life when He did not obey His mother's request. This was shortly after His ministry had begun. Crowds were thronging Him for healing and deliverance. His mother and family came asking Him to please come home as they thought He was out of His mind, or in the old-fashioned wording, "beside Himself"—He was taking His call too seriously and would get in trouble. Also, they probably expected Him to keep on taking care of the family in Joseph's place. His siblings had no doubt looked to Him as a substitute father as often happens with the oldest son.

The weaning process had to begin. Jesus did not comply with His mother's and family's request, but went on with His work, realizing they would eventually understand (Mark 3:21, 32–35). He knew He had to obey His heavenly Father over His mother's wishes. I'm sure it was not easy for Him, yet if He had obeyed His mother in this, there would have been no salvation for any of us, and that included His own family!

There are many accounts of Jesus getting in trouble for breaking the Sabbath by healing people, but He kept right on doing it! He was following His Father's directions, which superseded earthly laws. A number of times He said, "Moses told you . . . but I say unto you." Jesus was a psychologically healthy Person who didn't need to comply with public opinion, or even His family's opinions, but did what He knew was right.

Maturity Enjoined

Jesus was the most mature person who ever lived, and He can help us grow in maturity. As we learn to walk according to God's Word and Holy Spirit, the Maturing Adult within us will grow more and more into the stature of Jesus Christ. Saint Paul directs the believers at Ephesus as well as us to this goal: "till we all come to the unity of the faith and the knowledge of the Son of God, to a perfect man [complete adult], to the measure of the stature of the fullness of Christ: that we should no longer be children [Hurt

Children], tossed to and fro and carried about with every wind of doctrine, by the trickery of men, in the cunning craftiness by which they lie in wait to deceive, but speaking the truth in love, may grow up in all things into Him who is the head—Christ—" (Ephesians 4:13–15).

Look at the attributes of the Maturing Adult so you can see when you're functioning that way. He or she:

> gives and receives love freely
> affirms others
> is a good listener
> doesn't need to be critical in order to feel important
> is responsible at home and on the job
> looks for the best in others
> is a stable person
> isn't judgmental
> is confident
> has great joy in giving.

Not only was Jesus the most mature person who ever lived but at the same time He was the most childlike. We likewise need to remain childlike in the best sense of the word, as we grow in maturity. Our souls should function between the stability of the Maturing Adult and the freshness of the Creative Child. I've known people who function only from their Creative Child, and I've known some people who function only from their Maturing Adult. It's most effective and happy to live in balance between the two, as Jesus did.

In this age of computers, a computer example would be in order. The information you gather and store in the Hurt Child and the Prejudiced Parent can be processed by the Maturing Adult. The adult is much like a computer that looks at all the data, then makes a decision, but like a computer, the adult can only function in terms of what it receives. If anger comes in, anger comes out! Either the Maturing Adult will be able to process information and make

sound decisions or it will be insecure and damaged, making un-
sound decisions. If your parents have been relatively free from prejudices and other hang-ups and have taught you to make decisions
based on sound logic, the results will generally be good.

The adult-self, in a human being who doesn't know the Lord, is
not going to be able to save the situation totally on his own. "Do it
yourself" concepts fail without the help of the Holy Spirit as the
Programmer. The hope of the day is that by teaching people to be
calmly intellectual and objective, the ills of society will be cured.
But it's not much good telling people to be calm and reasonable on
a sinking ship! The intellect of the adult-self simply doesn't have
the kind of input it needs. That can come only from God by the
Holy Spirit.

Only God can help you adequately process and eradicate data
from the Prejudiced Inner Parent and the Hurt Inner Child, which
must be done if you're going to have a good voyage on life's sea. The
Prejudiced Parent and the Hurt Child need to be healed and transformed into the Maturing Adult and Creative Child. When we
became adults we were supposed to have ". . . put away childish
things," instilled prejudices, and other negatives (1 Corinthians
13:11). Guided by the Holy Spirit, the Maturing Adult and the
Creative Child within will assist you to do this.

This is one way to express how you can have peace with your
inner parent. As you read along, I will give you further ways to receive this kind of peace. I'm not saying it's easy to live in peace, but
I believe you're going to be successful because God, the great
Peacemaker, lives within you. He's pulling for you! As Jesus' Lordship grows in your life, and you learn to rely on Him, rather than
your parents, to give you what you needed in the past and need in
the present, you will be released from unhealthy ties to your parents. You can turn off that inner radio program which gives you
those negative and unhealthy directions and commands.

As you seek healing, God will assist in every possible way to help
you learn to love and honor your parents and be at peace with
them. You will become a peacemaker for yourself, your parents (or

the memories of your parents), and for your present family. You will be called "blessed."

The next chapter tells you further ways you can bless and be blessed . . .

Soul-Healing Prayers

Reliving Memories Wth Jesus Prayer. Assuming you have read Appendixes A and B (don't miss these steps), take some time to walk through a past scene with your parent(s), but before you do make sure you are aware of Jesus' Presence with you. Remember that though God was with you during the hurt, He doesn't control the wills of others, and was just as grieved about what happened as you were. As close to the original scene as you can, experience (feel, see, or hear) your omnipresent Lord Jesus. Let Him comfort you as you pour out any anger and hurt connected with this memory. Tell Him exactly how you feel so your emotions will not remain bottled up within you. (*Take your time.*)

Hear what Jesus would say to you to help you release the hurt and then to comfort you. If there was any sin on your part, confess it, and accept pardon from the Lord. (*Pause here.*)

Let those two great healing resources, God's loving *omnipresence* and *unconditional* love, heal you. Allow Jesus to do for you what you needed most at that time. (*Pause here. Take your time.*)

If the Lord gives you directions or new insights, or instructions concerning your parent or parents, write them down. Keep a journal of your prayer activities. As soon as possible begin to follow through where indicated.

Release From Prejudice Prayer. From your childhood memories, can you think of any prejudiced ideas your parents expressed or acted out toward you or others? (*You may want to write these down to make a progress report to check back on.*) Do you find that you also behave this way from time to time? Are you willing to give these impurities to God and keep only the gold? If your answer is *yes*, then pray the following petitionary prayer:

"Dear Father God, I ask You to heal me from wrong attitudes I've accepted from my parents or surrogate parents. I'm willing to be adult enough to let these childish thought patterns and behavior patterns be nailed to the Cross. You died so I could be free. I want to love as You loved and to let Your wholeness become a part of me.

"I ask You to remove from my life and emotions these prejudiced and critical attitudes from my childhood: (*fill in here*). Also any such attitudes I've added in my adult years (*fill in here*). Please take them away. Father God, I give you permission to go any level within me to heal, cleanse, and restore according to Your truth. I renounce every wrong teaching and attitude. Although it wasn't always right for me to obey my parent(s), yet forgive me when I didn't handle the situation in a way honoring to them.

"To the best of my ability, I invite You to be my Lord unconditionally. I know I can trust You and that You want the very best for me.

"Thank You, Lord God, in Jesus' name."

Forgiveness for Having Other Gods. Pray this prayer *if* it seems appropriate for you:

"Dear Lord, please forgive me if I have made an idol of my parent(s). Forgive me if I have made him/her a god in Your place. I know You want me to love my parent(s). Teach me to do it in the balanced way which is pleasing to You and healthy for us all. I will have no other gods before You. Thank You, Lord, in Jesus' name. Amen."

Chapter Five

Peace With Your Mother

For thus says the Lord,
Behold I will extend peace to her like a river,
and the glory of the nations like an overflowing stream;
then you shall be nursed,
you shall be carried on her hip,
and be trotted on her . . . knees.
As one whom his mother comforts,
so will I comfort you . . .

> Isaiah 66:12, 13 AMPLIFIED
> Words from the prophet Isaiah

Now the Lord of peace Himself
give you peace always
in every way . . .

> 2 Thessalonians 3:16

In your formative years, your mother was the most important person for your emotional security. You were very close to her psychologically during prenatal life and for the first eighteen months following your birth. That's why the loss of, or withdrawal of the mother's love, especially early in life, is one of the greatest deprivations a person can experience.

Some of us had the comfort of love from our mother while we were growing up, and some didn't. From some it was stolen by divorce, an angry or otherwise disturbed family member who preempted all the mother's attention, an ill or handicapped brother or sister needing most of the mother's care, or other such problems.

To love your mother and to know your mother are two different things. When a child, you depended on your mother to feed you and clothe you and take care of you in numerous other ways. You may, however, not have taken the time, or perhaps were not permitted, to know your mother intimately.

Dr. Harold Bloomfield, psychiatrist, interviewed in the May 21, 1984, *U.S. News & World Report* was asked: "How common is it for people to come to adulthood without really knowing your parents?"

He replied, "Very common. In my experience 90 percent of people say they have an incomplete relationship with at least one of their parents."

He was asked, "What price do people pay for a poor relationship with their father or mother?"

His reply was, "It can be very large. If we are carrying around regrets and resentments from childhood, it blocks our capacity to love and be loved. These unresolved conflicts also are often at the root of the anger and dissatisfaction that many of us feel, yet can't explain. It is largely through our parents that we come to form our attitudes about sexuality, friendship, love, success and money . . . the mark of an adult is the ability to take responsibility for your own happiness. If you blame others when things go wrong, that is a sign old wounds are not healed."

How I Got to Know My Mother

I don't think I truly got to know my mother, Loretta Ellen Reed, while she was on earth. I don't remember any significant conversations with her, nor for that matter, any angry words between us. She was thirty-seven when I was born, so by the time I was a teen, there was quite a generation gap.

She was the second child in a family of eight, and was raised on a small farm in the backwoods of Michigan. For lack of finances her education was cut off in the fourth or fifth grade. She was intelligent and capable, a beautiful young brunette with dimpled cheek, who in our day could have been a fashion model. At eighteen, my dad told me, she was five feet, six and a half inches tall, weighed 125 pounds, and was graciously proportioned.

My mother rarely talked about her childhood to me. Perhaps the memories were too painful. I learned most about her formative years from my father after her death, and by locating and talking with some of her immediate family I had lost touch with. My brother Bob, when he and his family visited us in 1981, told me more of my early history and that of my mother.

My mother's mother, my maternal grandmother, was an only child. While still in her teens, she ran away with the young man hired to take care of her father's horses and grounds. She was semi-disinherited for this, and partially as a result, her husband, my maternal grandfather, had a lot of anger, which he seems to have vented on his children.

An Abused Child

At the age of fifteen, my mother, Loretta, ran away from home following a beating by her father. She and her watchful dog walked two miles through a forest trail in the middle of the night to a country train station. A Methodist minister, his wife, and teenage daughter, who were in the process of moving to a new work in the Midwest, found her at the depot and took her under their care until she was almost eighteen, a modern example of the Good Samaritan! She trained as a practical nurse at the Methodist Hospital, where her surrogate father worked as a chaplain.

My brother Bob, a dental surgeon, describes her capabilities this way: "I recall how mother delivered two children for our poorer neighbors who could not afford a doctor. Pretty good for a farm girl with only a grade-school education!"

A Trip to Heaven

I was my mother's fourth and last child. Her health was poor. I always remember her being very overweight, and she was perhaps past the safest age for child-bearing. She came very close to death when I was born. In fact, she must have crossed over and come back, because at times she would describe to me how beautiful heaven was: "pearly gates and streets of gold," just as the Book of Revelation describes it. In fact, once she arrived in heaven she said she didn't want to return, but God sent her back to us.

In my childhood, I remember her saying to me, "Rita, I went to heaven to get you." I've since realized how sensitive and loving that was. She could have said, "I almost died when you were born"; or made the damaging, guilt-producing statement one mother made: "You almost killed me when you were born."

Today I am the smallest of the four children. I'm five feet, three and a half inches tall, and I weigh 125 pounds, but I weighed more than any of the others did at birth—a hefty nine pounds, seven and three-quarter ounces! I had little tires of fat around my legs and tummy. My mother must have eaten a lot during her pregnancy!

Praying for My Own Healing

After some years of praying with others for inner hurts, I thought I needed this kind of prayer myself. In any case, those praying with others for soul healing should experience what it's like to be prayed for. I asked Shade and Janet, my close friends, to meet with me.

We first prayed together through the months of my prenatal life, but they didn't seem to contain anything needing help. When we got to my birth, however, I told of my mother's experience of visiting heaven, and Shade was inspired to say, "Rita, at the time your mother died and came back you were still attached to her by the umbilical cord, so you must have experienced heaven along with her!" Shade's insight meant much to me.

I'd wondered sometimes how I could pray with so many others, many of whom had fewer early hurts than I did. I seemed to have an inner strength that I would not have expected in the light of my formative years. Perhaps it came from that little taste of heaven at my birth!

Childhood Memories

As we prayed and talked, I recalled what I felt was quite an unhappy childhood. Mother suffered from varicose veins in her legs, always seemed tired, and had undefined physical problems. Because of her poor health and for other reasons, I felt neglected.

Then my older sister, Georgia, and I got off to a bad start. She told me recently (1986) that she has forgiven me for being born! I was glad about this because sometimes you need to forgive someone for something they couldn't help, but yet which was painful to you.

"When Mom and Dad brought you home from the hospital," Georgia told me, "I had a bad cold and fever. Because of this, Mom would only let me see your feet; she kept your head covered for fear of infection."

Talk about negative bonding—this was it! It must have surely felt like rejection to my four-year-old sister. Then, to add insult to injury, I was put in the bedroom with our folks where she had been, and she, against her will, was "graduated" to the upstairs of the house with her big brothers. As a result of all this, although we are close friends today, my sister and I did not get along too well when we were growing up.

As I look back at my childhood, the best periods seem to have been my nine months of prenatal life and the first two years after my birth, during which my family and I were all together with relatives in Michigan.

Enjoying my nine months of prenatal life may sound funny to you if you are not aware of what Dr. Thomas Verny[1] calls "the secret life of the unborn child," and the extensive research being done showing that the prenatal child experiences many things that affect him or her in later days. I have found it's possible to relive that time in the Presence of Jesus so He can heal. You can do the same.

My earliest conscious memory is at age two, driving with my family down a winding, mountain road on our way to Florida. The armrests in the backseat of the 1936 Chevrolet were fairly large, and I would sit on one and fall off as we turned the corners, giggle with delight, and then get back on the armrest for the next curve. My sister, Georgia, and brother Bob, ages six and eleven, were with us. The only "casualties" on our trip were our goldfish, who survived in their fishbowl until we were near Atlanta, where we had a burial service for them!

My older brother Bill (William S.), who was thirteen, remained in Michigan to complete his schooling, and it was a year or more before my father, William H. Reed, could sell his business in Michigan and join us permanently in Florida. This separation from my father must have been hard on me and my family. After we came to Florida, except for a few rare visits from relatives, we were detached from other family roots. My brother Bob was an important masculine figure in my life during my formative years, until he went into the U.S. Army Air Corps when I was ten.

My mother had a pioneering spirit about her. Perhaps having to leave home when only a teen strengthened her to leave her Michigan relatives, pack us up, and head for Florida. It was a brave thing to do in 1936 near the end of the Great Depression.

I must have been a lot for my mother to handle, for she sent me to school when I had just turned five. Needless to say, I was the smallest child in the first grade. (Preschool was rare in those days.) Each day the teacher would ask me or my sister where my birth certificate was. Each day we would explain that it hadn't come in the mail yet! Meanwhile the teacher took a liking to me and literally carried me around in her arms. I still remember how one day she took me upstairs and showed me the classrooms for the big sixth-graders. She gave me a beautiful lace handkerchief, which I kept until it fell apart.

One day she asked me once again, "Rita, how old are you?" and this time I responded with a statement I'd heard my father make in jest. "I'm five at home, and six at school," I said. The members of the class laughed, and I guess the teacher thought it funny, too, because I was allowed to remain in the first grade. That teacher was one of the first persons (other than my parents) I remember feeling loved by.

My mother did not attend PTA meetings nor was she involved with my schooling during these formative years. Again, praying about this with my friends helped me realize that my mother's seeming neglect was not because she didn't love me but because she felt inadequate. Maybe, too, the idea of going to PTA brought back memories of her childhood, and how she had longed to finish her schooling but wasn't allowed to. I realize now she just didn't feel capable of helping me with my lessons or relating to the people in the PTA.

Because of my mother's physical exhaustion and poor health, by the third grade I had to learn to wash my clothes (by hand), iron, catch the bus to town, and shop for clothes by myself. Though this probably wasn't best for me at the time, it did help to make me a confident person and kept me from being emotionally dependent. During part of my childhood, my mother worked nights down the street from our home in a nursing home.

As I thought and prayed about my childhood, I made a list of positive and negative points regarding my mother and me which I'll give you here.

Positive Points

Prenatal

My mother was a Spirit-filled Christian, although she didn't
fully understand her childhood experience until many years
later.

She didn't smoke (smoking limits the supply of oxygen to
the unborn child).

She didn't indulge in alcoholic beverages.

She didn't take drugs.

Birth

She didn't believe in abortion. (Sometimes we forget to be
thankful that our mothers let us live.)

She breast-fed me (she had a good supply!), so I had the physical and emotional benefits of breast-feeding.

Perhaps most important, through her near-death experience, I
may have had an early taste of heaven!

Youth

Mother took me to church, where I heard about Jesus and
about the power of the Holy Spirit.

She frequently read the Bible, and gave me a respect for the
Scriptures.

She believed in the gift of physical healing through prayer.

Mother was nearly always there when I came home from
school.

She never used profanity.

She never abused me.

She encouraged me to develop my musical talent (piano, singing).

She somehow imparted to me the idea that I could accomplish whatever I wanted to.

She liked feminine things, ruffles and lace, and occasionally did some embroidering and sewing.

She taught me to be polite and respect my elders.

She didn't try to control me; she let me be my own person.

Perhaps as a result of these positive things, without any encouragement or adequate preparation to go to college, I did. I graduated and went into a profession, as my brothers and sister had done.

Negative Points

Prenatal

I was perhaps not planned for, as I was the last of four children, and my mother was thirty-seven when I was born.

Other

My mother was physically and emotionally abused as a child.

She was sickly and tired much of the time (perhaps in part from repressing old memories, which tends to eat up energy).

I felt my mother's inadequacies.

I was sent to school too early.

I had to fend for myself at an early age (although this turned to my good).

My mother sometimes forgot to celebrate my birthday. (I surmise she was rarely remembered on hers when she was growing up.)

I thought my mother was pretty and wished she would lose weight so I could show her off to my friends.

She showed little interest in my schoolwork or school activities (although this I now understand).

She didn't know how to play, either at indoor or outdoor activities, again probably because of her childhood.

She had limited social contacts.

Throughout elementary school and junior high I was taken to revivals at church, when I should have been at home studying. Many nights I fell asleep on a pew.

My mother, though very ill, was able to be at my wedding in 1966. The next year, on her seventieth birthday, Dennis and I sent her a dozen red roses. In response, she wrote the second poem I'd known her to write. She died three months later. Here is evidence of my mother's latent creativeness and her ever-constant love for our Lord and for me.

SOUL OF A ROSE

Twelve crimson roses came today,
From my son and daughter far away.
Each one was perfect as their love for me.
A rose so sweet, and I can see,
The wonderful souls so true,
Deep inside of you.
"A rose is a rose"; a rose with a soul so true
For I have waft the perfume of the soul of a rose.

Tender days have flown too fast
When all the children have gone at last.

Each one a chosen profession on life's path,
But fond memories I hold dear.

When the crimson roses in the garden path appear,
I shall know, dearest, that your love is near;
Just a "twinkle of an eye" away
My love forever will stay.
When I see the Crimson Rose
With the fragrance of the soul in that perfect day,
Not far away but near to you, my Dears, I will be,
When the Sweet Rose of Sharon I see.

In the fourth stanza, when she spoke of seeing the "crimson roses in the garden pathway," appearing to lead her out of this life to the next, she said, "I shall know, dearest, that your love is near." I wasn't able to be with her when she died, but rereading my mother's poem has brought more healing to me, and it comforts me to know that since mother and I are one in Christ, I was there in Him.

I've come to understand my mother much better since I've been praying with other people for soul healing. For example, after praying with women who suffered abuse in childhood, I understand how the abuse my mother received must have affected her.

Then, too, I've come to appreciate my mother better since I've received soul-healing prayer myself. Although I knew my mother loved me, circumstances in life stole my awareness of that love away for a long time. I knew it with my head, but I didn't know it on the level of my emotions. Now my mother's love has been restored to me.

Your Mother's Importance

A girl's mother is most important to her when it comes to accepting her feminine identity, just as a father is most important to a boy in accepting his masculine identity. Problems with gender identity usually come from poor relationships with parents. The fact that we do or do not find it easy to sense or accept our identity is neither something we can claim credit for, nor should be put down for. We simply need to know that God can heal this, too.

Since the mother's example is so important to her daughter, the father should affirm his wife, and encourage the daughter to admire her and want to be like her.

In spite of the limitations in my upbringing, my mother, and my sister, too, must have been good role models of femininity for me, for I have never had any problem with my identity. When growing up I always wanted to be more feminine than I was.

On the masculine side, a boy, when an infant, and later in his teens, should have a special love relationship with his mother, which will help to develop his capacity to respond to and love the woman he marries. If this was lacking, or hasn't been established through prayer, it will be virtually impossible for him to love his wife, ". . . as Christ also loved the church, and gave himself for it" (Ephesians 5:25 KJV).

If You Need Mothering

A grandmother can be a substitute parent for you, if as a child or an adult you need mothering. Or you can unofficially adopt a friend as a mother figure.

Choose a woman for a surrogate mother who has a healthy marriage, who is emotionally stable, with qualities you admire; one who is willing to help fill the gap in your life, and whose own children won't look upon you as a threat. Her husband must be in agreement and work together with her in the surrogate-parent role.

You may find your needs are such that you need more than one surrogate mother. This "multiple mothering" can be very helpful for a certain period of your life, if you need it. Then, too, one "mother type" person will have qualities that another doesn't, and one may be less busy than another.

A few words of counsel here to those who accept the role of surrogate parent(s). Be sure that you and your husband present a united front at all times to the person you are "parenting." Physical acts of affection for the emotionally famished, such as hugs, should be engaged in only when both husband and wife are present. Remember that healing for the emotionally needy person will not be accomplished purely by giving physical attention and love to him or her. There must be consistent prayer for soul healing, too, with people who know what they're doing. It will usually be best if surrogate parents don't try to be prayer-counselors at the same time.

Being parents "in Christ" is a very important ministry to the wounded but also requires much prayer and wisdom, as well as some discipline.

Gloria

Working out memories of my childhood was a mild process compared to the difficulties of some I have prayed with. Let me tell you about Gloria. When she came for prayer-counseling at a seminar, she explained to Ethel Lipscomb, the prayer team leader, and the two other team members that she couldn't love anyone, including herself.

She had been raped at the age of twelve. She hadn't known who her mother was and had lived in foster homes from infancy. When old enough to do so, she searched for and found her mother. She discovered her mother was a prostitute, which caused more hurt, and made her wish she had not located her. When she came to the seminar, Gloria had just extricated herself from an abusive situation with a man which had gone on for several years. Ethel described her as being a very unhappy and angry woman who was greatly depressed with life and reflected all this in her total attitude. Her emotional, spiritual, and financial needs were overwhelming, and the prayer team, knowing they would have only one opportunity to work with her, earnestly asked the Lord to direct them.

Ethel said to Gloria, "You have been treated very cruelly, but your unforgiveness has you in prison so God can't bless you."

Gloria replied, "I just can't forgive."

Ethel said, "I know you can't forgive in your own strength. After hearing your story, I'm having trouble myself forgiving the people who have hurt you! But do you *wish* you were willing to forgive?"

Gloria was desperate and willing to try most anything, so she said, "Yes, I can say I *wish* I was willing to forgive."

Ethel encouraged her to go through the list of people she needed to "will" to forgive, beginning with the easiest saying, "Lord I *wish* I was willing to forgive [here she named a person from her long list], but I can't do it in my own strength. Please help me." As she prayed about one person after another, Ethel could see a gradual change come over Gloria's face. Then the Holy Spirit showed Ethel that Gloria was now ready to forgive her mother. Ethel realized that of the prayer team of three, she herself was the one closest to the age of Gloria's mother. She felt led to say, "Gloria, would you allow me to step into your mother's role and ask your forgiveness on her behalf?"

Gloria looked surprised, hesitated, and then replied, "Yes." So Ethel moved her chair into a convenient position, took Gloria by the hands, looked into her eyes and began, "Please forgive me for *never, never* giving you any of the love you needed at any age. I should have taken you in my arms from the beginning but I didn't. I wish I could go back and kiss all the hurt places, the skinned knees, and other injuries. Forgive me that I wasn't there to do it."

Gloria began to sob, and as the tears rolled down her face, Ethel went on, "When you were ready to change from a girl to a young woman, forgive me for not being there to tell you all the things you needed to know. Please forgive me for all the ways I've wronged you over the years."

As Gloria continued to cry, Ethel took her into her arms. When she could, Gloria cried out, "Yes, I forgive you," and wept until all the deep sobbing and heaving of her chest and shoulders stopped, and the hurt was gone.

After a while, Gloria sat back, smiling and wiping her eyes, looking very relieved. "I feel a thousand-pound weight has fallen off me," she exclaimed. "I know what Jesus wanted for me today has been done!"

She went on, "Now I want to help others, especially children, but I'm afraid I'll be hurt and rejected again."

Ethel counseled her, "Gloria, why don't you consider doing it in the name of the Lord? Scripture says that you'll be blessed if you give a person even a drink of cold water in Jesus' name. If you do these things to others you're doing them as unto Him." [See Matthew 10:40, 42.]

"That helps a lot," Gloria said. "I think I can do it that way."

The next day when Ethel saw her, Gloria reported, "I can see my mother in a different light now, and I realize she had the same needs as I had. I understand her for the first time and I have compassion for her. I'm really glad I've found my mother!

"You know, Ethel, during the service at the church the following evening, Father George Floyd suggested we all think of a favorite Scripture and claim it for ourselves. I thought of Third John 2, which states that Christians will prosper as their souls prosper, and did what he suggested. I immediately started thinking, 'I wonder what God has in store for me now!'

"Because I was able to release the heavy unforgiveness against my mother, shortly after the seminar was over, as I prayed by myself one day, the Lord showed me that it was time to forgive the one who raped me. With the strength of the Lord I forgave, and knew that at last I was *set free!*"

Whether you had big problems with your mother, or small ones, God can help you be healed. It's never too late to get to know about your mother or actually to feel you know her, even when you've hardly spent time with her at all. Perhaps you were without your mother from birth or from childhood. Or perhaps you had your mother, but she was incapable of giving you what you needed. The Holy Spirit has ways of giving us understanding beyond our limited knowing. We need to let Him do for us what He alone knows we need.

A Word About the Abused Child

If you were abused in childhood, there are some special things to recognize as you pray. Often members of the family will not acknowledge child abuse when it is going on, nor do they want to discuss it later. The abused child may feel to blame for his own abuse, and may think, *If I had just done things differently my parent(s) wouldn't have abused me.* As a result, he may not face the issue and get the help he needs. Eventually he or she must face the situation and pray through it in order to overcome debilitation and reach his/her full potential.

Some children have not been abused physically, but verbally—they have been beaten with words.

There are four kinds of child abuse: 1) *neglect*; 2) *verbal abuse*; 3) *physical abuse*; and 4) *sexual abuse.*

If you were an abused child, and are now grown up, and out of your parents' home, you may still need to protect yourself *if your parent(s) have not changed their ways.* You may still run the risk of verbal abuse when you are with them. You may have forgiven your parent(s), and be truly learning to love them, but you are also learning—perhaps for the first time—to rightly love and respect yourself.

It is not wise to expose yourself to more damage. You may need to limit your direct contact with your parent(s). Write them loving notes, assuring them that you care. Remember them on special occasions with cards and gifts, and so forth. If you talk to them on the phone, have your mate or relative join you on a second line, so that they can help you out if the conversation gets heated. If you need to terminate the call, you can excuse yourself to get something off the kitchen stove, pick up a child at school, go to the store. When you are with them, try not to be with them alone.

Forgiveness Checklist

Before you pray, look over the following checklist to see where you may need to forgive your mother. Some items on this list are for men, others for women, and still others for men and women both. Mark a check in the parentheses by the statements that register with you.

For men:

( ) 1. You are aggressive and unduly angry with women.

( ) 2. You never affirm your wife in public but instead make cutting remarks, even though you do it in jest.

( ) 3. You may not beat your wife physically, but you beat her with abusive or harsh words and accusations.

( ) 4. You did not have a close, loving relationship with your mother when you were in your teens. You did not think of her as a most special woman in your life.

For women:

( ) 5. You don't enjoy being a woman or you have a problem identifying with your mother (or grandmother).

( ) 6. Your mother didn't give you proper instruction about your body, or gave you the idea that the physical part of marriage is bad, that sexual intimacy is to be "put up with" or is "dirty."

( ) 7. Your mother didn't show respect to your father, and frequently criticized him in your presence, damaging your ability to properly respect men.

For both men and women:

( ) 8. You don't *feel* (not just intellectually accept) that your mother was one of the first persons who truly loved you.

( ) 9. You can't forgive your mother on the level of your emotions, though you've tried.

( )10. Your mother didn't give you the love and affection you needed in childhood.

( )11. You have a lot of unhappy memories concerning your mother.

( )12. Your mother didn't trust you in your time of developing sexuality.

( )13. Your mother still controls your life in adulthood and won't let you go.

( )14. You feel threatened by women in leadership, and find it hard to resist putting them down.

( )15. Your mother was an alcoholic or drug abuser or in some other way her life-style caused you to be abused or neglected.

( )16. You'd just as soon have the world be totally male (or female).

Wishing You Wanted to Forgive

Gloria's story is, in part, an example of forgiving with the will. This is the first step you need to take, in obedience to the Lord, and to keep yourself under the protection of the blood of Jesus Christ. If you have not already taken this step, here is a suggested prayer for you:

"Dear heavenly Father, I come in obedience to You to forgive my mother. I choose to forgive her for any and all the hurts she may have knowingly or unknowingly caused in my life as I was growing up. I set her free of all blame, and I set myself free from any unforgiveness toward her, in Jesus name."

If you feel you cannot will to forgive, you can do what Gloria did. As you recall, she found it hard to forgive but she said, "I *wish*

I was willing to forgive." You can even pray, "Lord, I *wish* I *wanted* to *want* to forgive!"[2] If you open the door of forgiveness even just a crack, God can get His healing light into your life.

It may help reach your emotions more deeply, if you can picture what it would be like if your mother were whole enough to ask your forgiveness and then picture her doing this. If this is too hard to do, ask a friend you feel close to, and perhaps someone near your mother's age, who can prayerfully step into your mother's role and ask your forgiveness as Ethel did for Gloria. A "Bridging the Gap" ministry.

Gloria had been estranged from her mother from birth until she was finally reconciled as an adult. Though the wounds were extremely deep, there weren't the numerous hurts one might accumulate by living together over the years.

If you need more time than Gloria did to work through memories, the following prayer, and especially "Reliving the Memories" at the end of chapter 8, will be helpful.

Forgiving your mother doesn't mean you have to accept her past or present behavior as right, but that you want to obey the Lord so you can be a whole person. It doesn't mean you have to come under her control, or live under the same roof or be very close to her. Forgiving means you want the best for your mother and will work and pray to that end, but it also means you must do what brings you peace. "Let peace be your umpire."

In the next two chapters I'll be sharing with you a case study which extends over an eighteen-year period. Beth needed healing with both mother and father relationships. Join me as we experience together many of the prayer sessions that helped bring about her healing and victory, and kept her from ending her life. . .

Reflection and Prayers

Reflection. Since children are easier to forgive than adults, you may want to picture your mother when she was a child and forgive her from that viewpoint.[3] The time you are considering here is *before* your parent hurt you, so it's as though it didn't happen yet. Looking at this parent/child, ask Jesus to reveal to you *why* your mother had the problems she had. Ask yourself, "How do I feel about my mother in this scene?"

Try to find some photographs of your mother when she was young— child, teen, and/or adult. Or try to remember what she looked like when you were growing up.

If you were removed from your mother in infancy, and you've never seen a photograph of her, ask the Holy Spirit to show you a picture of her.

It's never too late to know your mother. After all, even if she died when you were born, you still had nine months of the closest imaginable contact with her.

What can relatives tell you about her formative years? (You may need to write letters or make phone calls and do a bit of research.)

What kind of childhood did your mother have? Was she loved by her parents? Did she feel loved and accepted by them? What may have caused her to be insecure? How did she relate to her family, and they to her? Did her brothers and sisters (if any) support and affirm her, or was there pretty constant competition between siblings?

Parent as a Child Prayer. Perhaps you can imagine your parent as a child, sitting next to you while you hold her hand, or even sitting on your knee with your arm around her. Consider what you've found out about her childhood. As you picture her, think about her beginning and why she grew up making the choices she did. Ask God for the gifts of compassion and understanding for her child-self. (*Pause here for a while.*)

As the Holy Spirit enables you to forgive, do so. Seeing your mother as a child, you might speak forgiveness something like this, "Through Jesus, Mother, I forgive you. I see your hurts and needs from infancy and childhood and how you've passed these hurts on to me. I was wounded by these things but I choose not to blame you for them any longer. I let these hurts go. I set you free from my judgment; Jesus has set me free and is healing me."[4]

(*It is healing to our emotions to speak forgiveness from the past scene. But since we are living in the present, it's best to speak this forgiveness through Jesus Christ.*)

Then pray, "Dear Lord, I send my love to my mother through You. Please tell her, 'Mother I love you.' Thank You, Lord, for helping me forgive her. In Jesus' name. Amen."

(If you realize your attitudes have been wrong, ask God's forgiveness for yourself at this time.)

If You Lacked a Mother's Love. If you don't have any good memories of your mother, or you were separated from her at your birth and so have no conscious memory of her at all, go through your prenatal life, practicing Jesus' healing Presence during those months when you were very close to your mother.

Prayerfully read Isaiah 49:1, Psalm 139, and Psalms 22:9, 10. (Later I suggest you read slowly through the Scriptures given for prenatal and natal prayer in my book *Emotionally Free* from page 173 through 181.)

The Scripture at the beginning of this chapter shows a picture of God meeting the need of a mother in your life. He says, "As one whom his mother comforts, so will I comfort you" (Isaiah 66:12 RSV). So look first to God, your Father, to meet your need for mothering, too.

When you think of your birth, know that Jesus was there with you. You are just what He wanted. When He looked into your eyes with eternal bonding as at the Creation, He said, "It is good." You are good in His eyes.

When on earth, Jesus received love from His earthly mother, Mary, and that "mother love" is now a part of Him.[5] From Him you can receive a mother's nurturing love. Take some time to receive the love that God the Son is wanting to give you. (*Lay the book aside and wait in God's Presence.*)

Chapter Six

Beth Makes Peace (Part One)

OMNIPRESENT SAVIOR

Christ within me, hope of glory,
Christ beside me to restore me,
Christ behind me and before me,
Christ, I worship and adore Thee.

Christ above me to watch o'er me.
Christ beneath me to support me,
Christ the Word is spoken to me,
Christ the Life is spoken through me.

Christ in past, in present, future,
Christ, the timeless One, is with me,
Christ my Peace, my joy forever,
Christ, my Omnipresent Savior.

RITA BENNETT, based on
Saint Patrick's Breastplate

But now in Christ Jesus you who once were far off
have been made near by the blood of Christ.
For He Himself is our peace . . .

Ephesians 2:13, 14

You're my last hope, Beth thought to herself as she took a seat in a conference room of the large auditorium. *If this doesn't work, I'm ready to give up on Christianity and I'll end my life.*

I met Beth, a young woman in her early twenties, one snowy evening in 1967, but I had no idea these thoughts were going through her mind. It's a good thing I didn't, otherwise I might have been distracted from the instruction I was giving a roomful of people.

My husband, Dennis, and I had been invited to her city to speak at an ecumenical seminar on the Holy Spirit. There was a snowstorm that winter weekend, but the people didn't seem to mind as they filled the auditorium. While the larger meeting was going on, I taught a workshop on the gifts of the Spirit, which was followed by prayer for those seeking help and more power from God.

I met Beth during the prayer time at the end. She was a young woman, twenty-one years old, and sat in the front row looking sad and discouraged. She had been talked into coming to the meeting by a fellow employee in the office where she worked. I could see a pretty girl, hiding behind beige horn-rimmed glasses and long auburn hair that nearly covered her face, ringlets cascading down the front of her drooping shoulders.

Later I was to find that Beth had an Episcopal background but in her elementary school days had become a Baptist. As a child she was so faithful in attending Sunday school that she had won two honor pins for perfect attendance for those two (almost three) years. Although her parents were not happy about her interest in religion, they did allow her to attend the church she wanted to.

The first of three children, Beth's relationship with her parents was one of rejection and insecurity. She was a sensitive child and took things to heart. When she was growing up, she was afraid to read the Bible in front of them, ever since her mother had taken away a Bible storybook she was reading.

She later told me, "One day, during this time, I was singing Christian songs around the house. After all, I had received Jesus into my life and He was Someone to sing about! Shortly after this my father said to me, 'If that's the only kind of song you can sing, then don't sing!'

"I never sang another song at home after that."

Beth was in great need that night we first met but she must have believed Jesus' words, "Blessed are those who hunger and thirst for righteousness, for they shall be filled" (Matthew 5:6). That night she received the release of the Holy Spirit and a new ability to praise God beyond herself. Her face was filled with joy as a new chapter in her life began. This helped to sustain her and to make her more open to receive help from the Lord later.

She came to visit us, and we explained to her from a biblical perspective the difference between her renewed spirit, which was joined to God's Spirit when she accepted Jesus, and her soul or psychological nature (intellect, emotions, and will), which was still in the process of being made whole.[1] This helped her because her moods varied widely.

During her early twenties, via long-distance telephone, we prayed her through learning to drive, moving out of her parents' home to be on her own, and getting a secure job. Off and on we saw her in person, when she drove up and visited us from her home 150 miles away. She was often discouraged and lonely. Her situation was as if she had been thrown a life preserver but still needed help swimming to safety.

New Hope

In the spring of 1979 I received a desperate phone call from Beth. "I don't think I can go on—or want to go on living," she said. "As you know, I've accepted Jesus, been baptized in the Spirit, had deliverance prayers, but nothing's working for me. I don't know what I'm going to do!" Then she repeated her often-heard phrase, "I'm bad."

In the previous year, along with my friend Shade O'Driscoll, I had begun to learn from the Lord some effective ways to pray for wounded souls. I had seen soul-healing make a profound difference for a number of people. A woman ready for a fifth nervous break-down was now well, able to sleep again, and cope with life. A young Christian man whose life had been affected by undiagnosed dyslexia in his childhood (a learning disability) was now released from depression and feelings of inadequacy. I felt it was the right time to give one more suggestion to Beth.

"Wait, Beth. Don't give up!" I said. "Jesus has more help for you. Let me tell you about soul-healing prayer. The Lord has done so much for you already, and looking back over the twelve years I've known you I can see the progress you've made, whether you can see it right now or not. Yet due to the hurts of your past, most of the time you can't feel or enjoy those blessings. God's Spirit, living in your spirit, is pouring out good things for you, but your wounded soul is blocking your mind and body from receiving and experiencing them.

"Soul-healing prayer is allowing the Holy Spirit to reveal Jesus to you and with you all through your life, and then through prayer letting Him be Lord of your past as well as your present. As you do this, your emotions will be healed so you can forgive everyone.

"Beth, it's been accepted in the Christian church for two thou-sand years that God is *omnipresent*. The entire Bible teaches that God is present everywhere and at all times. In Ephesians 1:4 Saint Paul says, 'He [God] chose us in Him before the foundation of the world, that we should be holy, and without blame before Him in love. . . .' That's saying God was in your past as well as being in your present.

"Because God is outside time, He can look down the corridors of time and see you choosing Him. He also chose you even before the earth, the animals, and first human beings were formed. He created your spirit, at the time of your conception; you then became a liv-ing soul. The good news doesn't end there. He's been with you all your life whether you've realized it or not.

"Let me say here," I added, "God's omnipresence is different from His indwelling presence. God is present *with* everyone, at all times and places, whether they have accepted Jesus or not. But He came to live *in* you, in your spirit, when as a child you obeyed Jesus' most important commandment, '. . . You must be born again' [John 3:7] and received Him as your Savior. But God was *with* you always, and by seeing God present with you, as well as in you, can assist Him in healing your whole life, past and present. God can't change your historical past, but you can allow Him to change your feelings about the memories of your past, and how they affect you today."

Prayer on the Telephone

I asked Beth what had happened recently to distress her. She was easy to evaluate. When she was upset and in her Hurt Child, her voice immediately gave her away. At these times she would sound like a sad little girl, not the young woman she actually was.

She told me how her close friend, another student who was several years older, had informed her that she never wanted to see her again. I was not surprised that Beth's deep need to be loved and insatiable need for physical affection would have taxed their friendship, but the rejection was real and painful nonetheless. I said, "Beth, let's pray about that memory right now over the telephone. You see Jesus knows all about how you're feeling. He was rejected above all people, as the prophet Isaiah describes so well, and Jesus deeply emphathizes with you." Then I asked her, "Can you picture the place where this occurred?"

"Yes, it was in a classroom. I can see us standing there."

"Ask the Holy Spirit to make you aware of Jesus' Presence with you."

She paused. "He's doing that. In fact, I can see Jesus there, and He's putting His arms around us both and reconciling us."

After waiting in silence for a time, she reported joyfully, "*That* certainly makes me feel a lot better!"

"Beth," I said, "I'm sure you've forgiven your friend from the present moment with your will, but now I'd like you to forgive her from the time of the incident Jesus has just healed. As you remember the scene, speak forgiveness from that time frame."

She was able to do this easily as I led her:

"[Naming the person], through Jesus I forgive you for rejecting me. It hurt me deeply, though I know you did what you thought best. You didn't know that I had a lot of other hurts in my past, which made your rejection seem bigger than it was. I forgive you and won't hold this against you any longer. I let the hurt go. Jesus is healing me."

I called her a few days later, and she was still happy about the results of the prayer.

Someone might say, "That sounds fine, but these women weren't reconciled in actual fact." Let me tell you what happened next. A month later, we were invited to speak at a meeting near Beth's home in Portland, Oregon. I talked about forgiveness. I knew Beth was there but didn't know her classmate would be there too. Following the meeting her estranged friend came up to Beth and me. I was introduced and then had the joy of hearing her say "Beth, will you please forgive me for handling things the way I did? I'm really sorry!"

Beth responded, "Of course, I will!" And truly Jesus was there with His arms around these two, reconciling them to Himself and one another.

I don't know if that excites you as it does me but I was absolutely delighted as I was allowed to watch the fulfillment of what we had seen God do "in the Spirit" a month before. When you and I forgive, we help set up conditions whereby the Holy Spirit can do great things. The Lord allowed me to be there at the time to encourage me, *so I could encourage you.*

This miracle did build Beth's faith to believe God could meet her other needs, although I knew it would take time.

Finding Time to Pray

I knew Beth would require much help, but saw from this initial experience she would be responsive to soul-healing prayer. Though it was a long drive, she was willing to come up to Edmonds as often as needed.

I prefer to pray once a week, or at least every other week, but because of the distance we decided for our first sessions to have Beth come up and stay for four days, so we could pray for an hour or two each day. Following that, we would meet as schedules allowed.

I asked my good friend and co-worker, Janet Biggart, to join me as a prayer partner. None of us knew that we were making a commitment to work together for six years, and that then, because of the increasing busyness of my traveling schedule, Janet, and a new partner, would be going on for an additional year. Don't let this long time concern you! It is not typical for counseling to continue over such a long period. We met on an average of five times a year. One year we didn't meet for prayer at all. If we could have met regularly, the whole process could have taken eight months or less.[2] On the other hand, we can see value in having prayed with Beth as the needs surfaced over the years.

What follows is a step-by-step picture for your instruction. You'll see some "reliving the scene with Jesus prayers" as we walked through Beth's wounded memories, and how those were followed by "forgiving from the emotions."

Here are many "creative prayers," when God shows what He had wanted for Beth in the past, and allows her to experience it.

(For further explanation of creative prayer—what it is and what it isn't—see my book *Emotionally Free*.)

Sometimes there's a combination of the two, or a "reliving and creative prayer."

There's a prayer for reconciliation between the adult Beth and the child Beth.

There are some prayers for deliverance.

There are prayers for confession of sins which were needed from time to time.

Our Team Meets for the First Time

Beth, now age thirty-two, arrived at our home on March 10, 1979, and I got her settled in the guest room. When the doorbell rang, signaling Janet's arrival, we went to meet her. I introduced the two. Janet, fair-skinned and brunette (at this time in her mid-forties), is a comfortable person to be around—a motherly type. A wife and mother of three, a former teacher, she is bright and insightful and I felt the right person to work with us. We sat down in the living room, on either side of Beth, and visited with her awhile. Then we asked her a few questions, which we've found helpful in deciding where to start praying. I asked, "Who is the first person you ever felt loved you?"

She pondered and replied, "Well, I know my parents must have loved me but I don't *feel* they did. I guess the first person I truly felt loved me was the friend we prayed about on the telephone, and you later met."

"You know, Beth," I said, "to be thirty-two and have had only *one* person you felt truly loved you, explains some of your severe depression. Thank heavens for one person who cared, but it's no wonder you felt so despondent later on when rejected. How wonderful now that she has offered reconciliation and received your forgiveness!"

Janet asked Beth another question we find very helpful: "What is your first hurtful memory?" Beth started to answer, but before she'd gone far she excused herself and went to her room, saying she had an upset stomach. We went to join her, and spent some time comforting her and praying that she would be bathed in God's love.

It seemed best to shorten our first visit, but before we said good-bye we planned our time to meet the next day, Friday.

Beth told me later, "That first meeting was hard for me because I didn't know Janet then. And then too, inner-healing prayer was new to me."

First Day of Prayer

March 11, 1979. Beth shared that her first and strongest hurtful memory was when she was rushed to the hospital for surgery, at age three.

"Since it was an emergency, my parents obviously didn't have a chance to prepare me for the situation. As I was given the anesthetic, I became hysterical. The nurse comforted me and told me I'd be okay, and as she consoled me, the anesthetic took effect.

"I had severe appendicitis. If they hadn't operated right away, I could have died. Yet to me the worst part about my ordeal was when, shortly after my hospitalization in the children's ward, a communicable disease (I think it was mumps) broke out among the children, and our parents weren't allowed to visit. I was separated from my parents for most of my hospitalization, which lasted five weeks."

"Five weeks!" I interjected, "That must have been terribly hard for you. Dr. Frederick Leboyer, the famous French obstetrician, says that children feel things *a thousand times* more intensely than adults. Adults often don't realize when they remember childhood hurts, which they now understand and can evaluate intellectually, that their child-self initially felt those hurts many times more than their adult-self remembers them. And those feelings may still be locked inside." I paused a moment, and then went on, "But tell us what happened during that separation."

"I guess I transferred my love from my mother to the nurse,

since during at least four of those weeks I didn't see my mother at all," Beth replied.

"Then to add to that, when I was ready to come home I felt rejected by her again, because my father was alone when he came to pick me up at the hospital. My brother was just a baby, and my mother had to stay home and take care of him. Of course, being a three-year-old, I didn't understand."

"As we pray, try to get into your childhood feelings and express how you would have felt then," I said. "As an adult you may have forgiven people in the memories we'll pray about, but your child-self may need to forgive from your emotions of the past. We'll give you opportunities to do this as we go along."

I stood up and moved from my chair to join Beth and Janet on the couch, and Janet moved closer too. We knew Beth was a Christian, and had never been involved with cults or occult, so this didn't need to be dealt with before praying. We joined hands, Janet asked God to show Beth where He wanted the healing to begin, and asked the Holy Spirit to lead us, guide us, and protect us. (We always start by praying like this, although for brevity's sake I won't always mention it.) We asked Beth to describe to us what the Lord was showing her and saying to her, and any feelings that might surface.

After a little time Beth said, "I'm remembering the operating room with very bright lights, and it's very frightening. I am being given the anesthetic but I'm not totally under when I hear the doctor who was to operate on me say, 'She probably won't make it.' Although the nurse tries to comfort me, the doctor's statement frightens me terribly, but now the fear is melting away because I know Jesus is there and I can feel the comfort of His Presence. I hear Jesus saying to those trying to help me, 'She's going to make it.' I guess for years I've felt that 'I'm not going to make it.' Do you think this feeling could have gotten started at that time?"

Janet and I nodded. An adult's word is law for a little child; a doctor's word would have had even greater impact.

"Though the doctor thought you were anesthetized,"[3] said Janet, "still it would be good for your inner child to forgive him for his words. This time why don't you follow me as you speak forgiveness from your child heart?"

"That would help," said Beth.

"Do you remember the doctor's name?"

"No, I don't."

"That's okay, we'll just call him 'doctor.' God will know to whom you are referring."

"Doctor who operated on my appendix [Beth repeated each phrase after Janet]. . .

"You didn't mean to, but in your concern you spoke your thoughts aloud . . .

"And frightened me when I was already terribly frightened . . .

"You didn't realize that this would be harmful to me . . .

"Through Jesus I forgive you . . .

"I choose to let this hurt go. I won't hold on to it any longer . . .

"Jesus has healed me . . .

"Thank you for being God's instrument to help save my life!"

There was a pause. "Now the Lord is showing me," said Beth, "the children's ward where I was confined so long. I see Him there comforting me and playing with me; He's holding His arms around my chest, holding me very tightly and close, while He swings me back and forth, my feet hanging free . . . Now He's letting me know that the nurse who was so kind to me was a special gift, but that she shouldn't replace my mother. He's holding me in His arms and letting me know that He will heal these memories of early separation from my parents."

I spoke up, "Beth, when you are by yourself before bed tonight I think it would be good to pray through your memories of separation from your parents, reliving those scenes, but this time practicing Jesus' Presence with you.

"As we finish praying this afternoon, it would also be a good idea to forgive your mother from your child-self. The nice thing is you can do this without going and telling her face-to-face that you forgive her. That might hurt her feelings and she might think you were being ungrateful for all she had done."

"That's true," Beth replied, "it would surely turn my mother off."

"Then let's speak forgiveness once again."

"What did you call your mother?"

"Mom."

Beth hesitated. "Can I put my head on your shoulder as I do it?"

"Sure," I replied, and so she did. I went on, Beth following me:

"Mom, through Jesus . . .

"I forgive you for not coming to see me in the hospital . . .

"I didn't understand that you couldn't visit me . . .

"And I forgive you especially for not picking me up at the hospital when it was time to come home . . .

"I was afraid that you didn't love me . . .

"I felt you rejected me . . .

(*Beth by herself*) "And my little sister had replaced me . . .

"I let these hurts go . . .

"I won't hold on to them any longer . . .

"Jesus is healing me!"

"You know," Beth said lifting her head from my shoulder and looking up at us for a moment, "I think *I* need to ask God's forgiveness." With eyes closed again, "Dear Father, I ask You to forgive me for rejecting my mother because I *thought* she had rejected me. I did to her what I thought she had done to me. Forgive me for the anger and resentment I've held in my heart against her. And please forgive me for any jealousy I had in my heart against my little brother at this time. In Jesus' name I pray."

Taking her hand, I spoke forgiveness from God's Word. "Beth, the Scripture says in First John 1:9, 'If we confess our sins, He is faithful and just to forgive us our sins and to cleanse us from all unrighteousness.' Since you've been obedient to what God's Word proclaims, you are free."[4]

Beth looked up and smiled, "I feel so much better! Do we have time to work through two more things? I think I need to forgive my mom for not understanding the insecurity I felt when we moved to a new location."

Janet and I said yes, and we prayed about a seven-year-old's memory of moving to a new area. Children, especially if they're insecure, can find moving very difficult.

Then we prayed about a nightmare she had when she was ten. She couldn't recall the actual dream, but she woke up, frightened, and wanted her mother to sit with her till she went to sleep again, which her mother didn't do. As Beth relived the memory, she knew Jesus was sitting by her bedside. He took her fear away and stayed with her until she was asleep.

She forgave her mother and prayed, asking Jesus to let her have a mother's love. In a creative scene she saw herself at age three and her mother holding her just as Jesus had, her mother's arms around her chest, holding her very tight and close, while she swung her back and forth, feet hanging free.

In creative-healing prayer, the Holy Spirit allows our emotions to receive what we were actually deprived of. The Scripture in 1 Corinthians 1:28 describes it this way, "...God has chosen ... things which are not, to bring to nothing the things that are." Or another verse tells about, "... God who gives life to the dead and calls those things which do not exist as though they did" (Romans 4:17). Through our prayer and His gifts, God can give us what we didn't originally receive in childhood.

March 12, 1979. The next concern which surfaced was Beth's hatred of her body at age ten.

"My feminine traits began to develop early, and I remember boys teasing me at a neighborhood playground, at school, and at home."

"You know Beth," said Janet, "most girls at puberty get teased like this, and some find it flattering. For some reason you were more sensitive and took it seriously. Let's pray about it, and let

Jesus heal your embarrassment. Can you see Jesus anywhere in this memory?"

Beth responded, "There's no one I can run to for help. I'm not close enough to my mother to talk to her, and I certainly can't go to my father. But now I see Jesus coming to me while I'm at the playground. He's seeking *me* out. His eyes are filled with love as He looks at me. He's taking me on His knee and holding me. The greatest thing is I can feel His love as He looks at me. Now He's telling the boys who are standing close by not to be mean to me and He's forgiving them for hurting me. Since He's forgiven them, it makes it easier for me to forgive them also.

"It's hard for me to reveal these feelings since I've never told anyone before. But it feels good to let go of the burden."

One of Beth's great desires was for a woman at least ten years older than herself to hug and hold her. This was an all-consuming craving which she often daydreamed about, and we knew it was a symptom of having been deprived of her mother's love, at birth, in the hospital at age three, and many other times. Her emotional growth had been checked at an early age.

Often a memory and the accompanying emotions will be totally healed in one time of praying. At other times, there will be some release, but the person will need more prayer. Then too, it may be some time needs to elapse before the person is ready for God to work more deeply.

In these early years of working with Beth, her need for holding was so great, that except for hugs of greeting, we had to limit other hugs with her to our prayer time with the three of us together. (Her healing eventually made it unnecessary for us to have to ration long hugs!)

Before we finished praying that day, Beth told us about an area of personal guilt which made her feel as she put it, "bad and unworthy." When she was twelve, she and a girl cousin had done some sexual experimenting. This is where Beth had learned to masturbate. We prayed about this, and the Lord said He was glad that she was interested in knowing about her body, because it was special, but that they had gone about it in the wrong way.

Children and teens with difficult home lives may use masturbation as an emotional escape. An excess or compulsion here shows need for healing. A compulsion coupled with fantasy can be tool for demonic activity. The enemy tries to get a controlling hook into our sexual lives very early on, if possible.

Janet and I were in surrogate-parent roles, explaining things to Beth which she should have known years before.

I asked her to *keep a prayer journal* along with me. In it she would describe her feelings at the end of each time together.

Beth's Journal Begins. When it was time for Janet to go, I didn't want her to leave. I suddenly wanted to be very bad. I wanted to hang on to her and not let her go, until she would be so angry with me that she would reject me. But for some reason, I let go before this happened. After Janet left, I hurt inside so much and I was very angry.

God showed me I was angry because I had not completed the cycle of forcing someone who cared about me to reject me, thus reestablishing the image I have of myself that says I am unworthy and no one could love me.

I went out for a walk. I also wanted to run away from the Bennetts' home to make Rita angry, so she would reject me, but I couldn't do it. I just kept thinking how much it would put them out if I didn't get back.

March 13, 1979. I shared with Rita and Janet about the first psychiatrist I went to. When I was twenty-three, one of the many women I "idolized" was a social worker. She was concerned about me because of my deep depression and suggested I see a medical doctor. With much coaxing on her part, I went to the doctor, but he could find no physical reason for the depression and the pain that I felt in my body. I later discovered the pain was emotionally induced.

When I told my friend the results, she suggested I see a psychiatrist. I wouldn't have done this for anyone else but I wanted to please her. Also she was going in the hospital soon for some surgery, and I didn't want to upset her at such a sensitive time.

I saw my first psychiatrist probably ten times. At the end I felt he betrayed my trust by asking my parents to come to one of my appointments without telling me beforehand. He also told them things I didn't want them to know, because I thought they wouldn't understand. He persuaded me to move out of my parents' home, which I did.

When I called home my mother said, "Your father is so mad at you he doesn't want to talk to you or even have you visit us." With Rita and Janet's help, I forgave the psychiatrist for betraying my trust. I forgave my mother for telling me about my father's rejection, and then I forgave my father.

I stopped going to this psychiatrist and went to another one that I had more rapport with. I saw him for a year. His basic method was hypnotherapy, which only temporarily relieved my psychological pain and helped me cope. It didn't remove the cause of my problems, and the pain returned a short time after each session.

Sometime after this, some other Christians prayed about my submission to hypnosis, and had cast away any wrong influence from the experience. Now Janet and Rita prayed that I would not be tempted to use hypnosis, or escape into it for relief from my pain.

Some years later when I was twenty-eight, I went to two group-therapy sessions, each being six to eight weeks at a time. In the group we had done some role playing. The leader saw my fear of men, and asked me to sit on a man's knee. This was so upsetting to me that I realized I must have repressed the memory of an unhappy experience with a man at some time, but I couldn't get the memory completely to the conscious level during my time in group therapy.

Now in the loving atmosphere with Janet and Rita I could fully recall what had happened. I remembered that when I was nine years old, a family friend had fondled my body while I was sitting on his knee, which made me feel dirty. As I shared this memory I really sobbed. I asked Jesus to hold me but I couldn't feel Him there. I saw Him come in the form of a very bright light. Although I couldn't feel Him holding me, He gave me His peace, and I stopped crying.

Rita then helped me speak forgiveness to the man from the emotions of my nine-year-old self. "Through Jesus, I forgive you for taking advantage of me. You caused me to be afraid of men and unable to trust them. I choose to let this hurt and disillusionment go. I forgive you in Jesus' name, and I won't hold this against you any longer. Jesus is healing me."

[Praying about this repressed memory at nine was a breakthrough for Beth. She had come to realize the unconditional love of God and so was open enough to let the memory surface. Now she began to experience new freedom.]

March 14, 1979. Riding home from Seattle on the bus, I kept seeing (in my mind) my mother holding me when I was three. But mostly I saw Jesus holding me (as described before) and sometimes tickling me until I laughed. The laugh was joyous and contented. When I arrived home, I felt really loved, and I wanted to love others as I had been loved.

I joyfully began to realize that inner-healing prayer not only helps you cope with life but goes back to *where there is pain and heals it.*

As I tell about our prayers with Beth, realize there were times of being upset, times of tears, times spent in waiting, and times for holding Beth (sometimes for as long as five minutes). We usually ended prayer sessions with a "holy hug" with the three of us together.

Not all people are as visual as Beth was. She moved in creative prayer easily, and as she experienced good results, it became even easier. She was not as open in her ability to *hear* from the Lord at first, but this increased as her confidence in her relationship with Him grew.

August 1979. In August Beth called to make an appointment for more prayer. I set up a two-day session. I asked if there were any results so far, and she said, "Yes, I don't feel the need to be held as much. I still want to be, but the driving force has lessened."

A Series of Harassments

August 25, 1979 (Rita's Notes). In our first session that Saturday I asked Beth if she had any other memories to pray about, like the fondling incident.

"Yes," she said, "I do remember a man trying to pick me up in his car when I was about ten or eleven and was walking to a Girl Scout meeting. I refused but he continued to follow me for about a block until I ran into school. I never told anyone about it."

Recalling this memory caused her to cry and say, "Why don't they leave me alone?" We comforted Beth and got out the facial tissues to assist in catching the falling tears.

The Holy Spirit led into a creative prayer. Beth saw the always-present Lord Jesus with her, and said she could see Him walking her safely to school. It was interesting that with Jesus there, the man never appeared. This is of course exactly what the Lord had wanted for His child.

She forgave the unknown man from the time of the original event and claimed freedom from any negative effects. She prayed for the man to be healed and come to Christ.

Beth then remembered a time in her early twenties, when a man on a bus fondled her. She remembered this happening on the bus several times, with several different men. *At that time, she was so passive she didn't know how to stop them.* She later avoided the problem by riding the bus standing up!

Seeing an obvious pattern here, I said to Beth, "Once a person has been sexually abused, it can make them more vulnerable to sexual advances, which is exactly what you're describing. Sometimes a seducing spirit has attached itself to the person, and prayer is needed to break its effect."

"It's sort of like this," said Janet. "Say that you were in elementary school and someone made a sign which said, KICK ME. For a joke they came up, patted you on the back and stuck the sign there. When people started kicking you, you wondered why they were doing it! Being molested as a child has very likely made you more vulnerable."

With Beth's consent, Janet led her in binding and casting away any seducing spirit that might still be harassing her. Janet asked her to follow and pray phrase by phrase: "Seducing spirit that harassed me in my past, if you have any influence on me at present, I bind you under the blood of Jesus and command you to leave me alone, in Jesus' all powerful name. Amen."[5]

We both then laid our hands on Beth's head and asked the Holy Spirit to fill and bless her.

August 26, 1979. As we mentioned before, the first person Beth felt loved by was the friend we had prayed about on the telephone. Because of the important place she played in Beth's life, the memory needed more work. Beth came to realize that some of her feelings about her friend were extreme and not what the Lord wanted. We encouraged her to talk to the Lord about these feelings. Prayer is talking to God and then listening. So we encouraged her to pray, then wait for an answer and tell us what she felt the Lord said.

Beth's Journal Continues. I told Jesus, "I want a good, deep relationship with my friend." He said, "I know but you can't have that." I told Him, "You don't care how I feel, and I don't like it here on earth anyway." He told me, "I didn't like it either but I had a work to do." I told Him, "I want to go to heaven," but Jesus said, "You must stay here because I have a special work for *you* to do." He told me, "Your stay on earth would be happier if you spent more time with Me."

[It took time for Beth to receive these words from the Lord. We felt as she relayed them to us that they were certainly from God, and were in keeping with His Word and His character as revealed in Scripture. We affirmed her in her ability to hear from Him.]

Janet prayed with me about hating myself, and that I would learn to love myself. She told me that when I sin and ask God's forgiveness He forgives me right away, but I also need to *forgive myself* right away.

Rita's Notes. The next concern was an incident with her mother. One evening when she was about thirteen, she came home late and her mother called her a "tramp." It made Beth so angry that she said, "Stop calling me that, or I'll become one." Beth told us she never was a loose person morally; in fact she had never had a date until she was twenty, and that was about it as far as dating was concerned. It was the least concern her mother needed to have had.

Breaking Inner Vow and Word Replacement

I led in prayer, asking Jesus to heal this memory. First of all, Beth renounced the inner vow to get even with her mother. Then we did a "word replacement prayer." She prayed after me, "In Jesus' name I bind the name 'tramp,' and I command any wrong influence from it to leave me." Then we laid our hands on her head and I prayed. "Dear Lord, please replace this destructive name with what You choose to call Beth. Help her see herself as you see her."

We waited, then I asked what the Lord was saying. She said, "I heard the name 'precious' but I find it hard to believe that Jesus would call me that!" We noticed that the word "precious" speaks of something expensive and valuable, such as precious stones or jewelry. It is just the opposite of the name "tramp," which implies being worthless.

I then encouraged Beth to "will" to forgive her mother. Beth said, "I don't want to be like her."

I answered, "That's fine, but you still need to forgive, or you may become like her."

Beth then asked God to help her be willing to forgive her mother. Without this forgiveness, the following prayers would have been blocked. We then prayed and asked Jesus to lead her into the memory where her mother had called her a bad name.

Scene Healed With Mother

Reliving—Creative Prayer With Mother. Beth told us that as Jesus came into the scene, He went up to her mother and just held her in His arms. This was upsetting to Beth because she wanted Jesus to hold *her.* Yet she didn't feel she could ask Jesus to come and hold her instead of her mother. Jesus held her mother for quite some time, perhaps three or four minutes. Janet saw the reason Jesus went to her mother first. It was in order that her mother could be healed so she could love Beth.

Beth then saw her mother prepare a beautiful dinner for Jesus, and when they had finished dining, He waved good-bye to her mother and came to Beth to hold *her.* We encouraged her to take all the time needed to receive the love Jesus had for her.

I never rush the time when Jesus is showing love to a person. This is where the reservoir which, with many, has been bone-dry now gets filled. Without receiving the love of God, the person will continue to seek love from human beings, which will never totally satisfy or fill the inner emptiness. Beth then *forgave* her mother *from the time of the incident* and told the Lord she wanted Him to have His way in her mother's life and in hers, too.

August 26, 1979 Later that day. (Beth's Journal). On the bus trip home I felt really clean and good inside. I felt like one of those ads for Ivory soap where they show a clean, wholesome-looking girl. Even when I got to the city and had to walk through the grubby part of town to catch another bus, I felt good. If a creepy guy came near me, I just reminded myself that I had been set free from being vulnerable to a seducing spirit and therefore no one would bother me, and no one did! Thank you, Jesus!

August 27, 1979. For some reason I feel really angry and depressed. I want to die. I feel like a pest to everyone. It would be better for everyone if I was dead.

August 28, 1979. I phoned Janet because I was extremely angry inside but didn't know why. We came to the conclusion that it might be caused by breaking my negative self-image, which says, "No one can love me." Janet prayed and in her prayer mentioned the name Jesus had given me, *precious*. With this I felt myself get very angry inside, and I told her this.

Homosexual Concern

April 2, 1980 (Rita's Notes). Today Beth shared that someone had told her that her need to be held by an older woman meant she was homosexual. Beth had never taken part in homosexual activity, and we talked about the danger of labeling people. We helped her forgive the well-meaning friend.

As a kind of "aside" here, I would like to quote for you, the reader, from *The Healing of the Homosexual* by Leanne Payne, which hadn't been published at the time we were praying with Beth. "One of the first things to do with the man (or woman) fearing there is no hope or healing for his deep gender confusion is to assure him that there is no such thing, strictly speaking, as a homosexual (or a lesbian). There is only a *person* (an awesome thing to be), created in the image of God, who is cut off from some valid part of himself. God delights in helping us find that lost part, in affirming and blessing it."

Prayers for School Days

Reliving—Creative Prayers

Beth's Journal. We reviewed what God had done for me thus far. Today we prayed about the school, where I felt really alone. I had to go to school by myself. In my prayer I saw Jesus going to school with me, so I didn't have to go alone anymore.

Next we prayed about the school where I got bad grades. The teacher wasn't there, and Jesus was the teacher. It was fun to be at school with Jesus, and it was easier to learn. I forgave the teacher for the way she treated me.

Then we prayed about the school where I was put back a grade. This time Jesus was in the classroom beside me and He bent over my desk teaching me how to write.

Rita reminded me of the Scripture in Romans 8:28 ". . . all things work together for good to those who love God . . ." and asked what I could see that was good in being put back a grade. One thing was I wouldn't go into the next grade without the basics and fail. The other was that I want to help children who have problems learning and I can understand how they feel.

Prenatal and Natal Prayer

Beth's Journal April 3, 1980. Today we prayed about my prenatal life and my birth. Rita led the prayer and asked me to stop her if at any time I had an insight or feeling I thought should be shared. She also asked Janet to do the same. She gave meaningful Scripture and prayers for each month.[6] I enjoyed everything until we arrived at my seventh prenatal month. Here I stopped Rita and said, "I feel my mother wanted a boy rather than a girl. I feel so rejected and lonely that I don't want to live."

We took extra time at this point, and I felt the Lord showed me that my mother wanted a boy because she rejected the feminine side of herself and wasn't happy with her own identity. Rita led me in speaking forgiveness to my mother from this time in my past. I didn't want to forgive my mother, and without Jesus' helping me, I wouldn't have succeeded.

While we prayed about my birth, I realized it must have been difficult as I felt claustrophobic. We bound the spirit of fear, and Jesus gave me peace. When I was born, Jesus was there in a white gown and He held me in His hands. As He looked at me, I knew He loved me. When it was time to go home from the hospital, Jesus handed me to my parents, and I could see myself as we drove home—my mother holding me.

Disillusioned

Dr. Charles Mangham, child psychoanalyst, says that when an adult is depressed to the point of suicide, it is a good idea to ask if he was ever greatly disillusioned by his or her mother.[7] I have found this to be helpful. When I asked Beth this question, she described a memory that had greatly bothered her.

From Beth's Journal (Reliving the Scene With Jesus Prayer). I was asked when my mother disillusioned me. I knew how to answer this right away. It was when I started my first menstrual cycle, and my mother broke my confidence by telling others about it. I was really upset and didn't want to forgive her! I saw Jesus in the room with His hand on my shoulder, comforting me.

When it came time to forgive my mother, I was sitting on His knee, leaning against Him. My mom came into the room. I told her I forgave her for not keeping my secret. Then I jumped off Jesus' knee and ran over and hugged my mother, and I felt real love for her.

Jesus showed me the reason mom told others this news was that she was excited that I was growing into a young woman. Janet said, she felt too, that my mother had difficulty keeping secrets because it made her feel important to be able to share the latest news.

You've seen from these accounts that hurts with Beth's mother were numerous and went back to her very beginning. The roots of her disillusionment came very early but the one at puberty was the culmination of all the rest. This is a tender time which should be handled with care. Beth's previous experiences with molestation would have made her overly sensitive to feeling exposed publicly.

April 4, 1980. (Rita's Notes). Beth wanted to talk about her problem of masturbation which was coupled with fantasy. We prayed for her release from this compulsion realizing the root cause would be healed completely as we continued our prayers together.

The most damaged people I've prayed with had several things in common. *First, they didn't feel loved by anyone in their childhood, some not until they were grown up; a few not at all. Second, they had fantasies to help them survive childhood.* Some were harmless, like creating their own imaginary worlds, and so forth. Others were destructive, often hooked into compulsive masturbation. *Third, these fantasies and sexual hookups were carried over into adult life.* If a person fits all three of these categories, including having destructive fantasies, healing will take time, commitment, and *agape* love from those called to pray with him or her.

Healing With Her Father

Beth's Journal. Even though I was very close to my father when I was a child, I had pretty much turned all men off since I was nine. Now I began wanting to be free to love my father. We broke the power of the command we realized my mother had given me, "You shall not love your father or any other man." I asked Jesus to reprocess these words and bring them into submission to the Holy Spirit. Jesus spoke to me and said He had been waiting for me to do this. A breakthrough!

Sandbox Memory, Age Three

Reliving the Scene and Creative Prayer. God gave me an idea that didn't seem to make any sense. I remembered when I was three and was playing in the sandbox with some friends. I dirtied my pants because I was having so much fun I forgot to come in. Mother spanked me very hard.

I relived the memory with Jesus as Lord of my past. This time Jesus carried me to my mother. My mother was mad at me but Jesus spoke to her and said He would change me.

Jesus cleaned me up and then held me. I couldn't feel His love but *I had peace* and for the first time in a long time *I didn't hurt inside.*

I forgave my mother, and we bound the idea that I was dirty, bad, and did everything wrong. We asked the Lord for a healing word, and He called me His daughter and said that I was pure and holy. It was hard to believe at first. Even now as I write this it's a bit hard, but I feel different inside. I feel clean!

(When a memory surfaces that doesn't seem to make sense, it is often a breakthrough. It may be something that happened so early and was so hurtful the person forgot it. The Holy Spirit brings it to mind at the right time.)

We always learn when we pray with people because we depend on the guidance of the Holy Spirit. During these difficult childhood memories, Beth often couldn't see Jesus until we let her hold on to one of us. Sometimes she had her arms about Janet's neck and sometimes mine, or had her head in a lap. Christ's love in us, joined with our love, helped her pray through these significant memories.

We prayed again October of 1980, and about a year later in the fall of 1981 Beth went back to college. We met with her only twice that year. Her return to school showed she was becoming more confident, yet many times it was hard for her to concentrate since she was still working through her problems.

December 4, 1981 (Operation Scene Prayer Repeated—Rita's Notes). The memory of the operation when three years old came back to Beth again with intensity. Her inner child felt that the operating team was trying to kill her. The Lord showed Beth that they weren't trying to kill her but that she herself wanted to die. We prayed that Jesus would give her hope for living and bound and cast away any *death wish* that influenced her when a child and now also as an adult.

Creative Prayer and Reconciliation Prayer

December 5, 1981. We discussed with Beth that she needed to work out her feelings of rejection, and to lean more on God for affirmation rather than on people. She had met a woman a little older than herself whom she admired, and was trying to figure out how to have a balanced friendship with her. Because she sometimes still wanted to be held, she had a recurrence of feeling she must be a "bad" person.

Beth's Journal. As we prayed about my feeling of badness, the Lord showed me that I was pure and holy. I saw myself dressed as a bride, pure and spotless. Janet saw a threshold like in a new couple's home. Jesus, dressed in white, carried me over the threshold and showed me numerous children—in wheelchairs. There was a sea of faces. I loved them so much it hurt terribly.

Janet asked, "Are there any children not in wheelchairs?"

I answered, "Yes, just one . . . and . . . it's me. She's so sweet and cute and is about two or three years old."

I bent down and picked her up and cuddled her. I asked why others didn't love such a cute little girl. I then realized others would love her as *I* continued to love her.

We then prayed a prayer of acceptance of my child-self. Big Beth spoke acceptance to Little Beth so that she could live and grow. And Little Beth, in turn, accepted Big Beth.

Progress Report

January 30, 1982. (Rita's Notes). Beth talked with Janet and me about how things were going at school. We tried to help her cope with the difficulties, and advised her on developing good study habits. She said, "Sometimes I still don't feel like living; however, I don't say 'I'm bad' anymore. I do still feel like a failure, though." We noted that Beth's picture of who she is and what she's like has greatly improved, but her idea of what she can do still needs help. However, the second problem is the lesser of the two.

Reliving the Scene Prayer (Beth's Journal). I've been thinking a lot about my childhood and I remember one incident that may have increased my fear of men. When I was four years old, I was playing at the next-door neighbor's house, and I saw him whip my six-year-old girl friend very hard with a belt. My girlfriend was screaming, and I was very upset. Her mother came home, and I ran to her. She picked me up and soothed me. She yelled at her husband for what he had done.

I don't remember many details, except that from then on, as a child I wouldn't go near that man. He tried to be nice to me, but I wouldn't have anything to do with him.

[Beth still didn't want to forgive the neighbor, but she was willing to pray an "I wish I wanted to want to" prayer.]

As we prayed about this memory, Jesus was with me holding my hand and then took me up into His arms and held me. Then Jesus picked up my girlfriend and washed her legs and healed her. He then carried us outside.

Jesus sat with the neighbor in the living room. He knew that he had been totally unloved as a child himself, and Jesus let him know that He loved him, though He wasn't pleased with his actions.

When I saw Jesus was willing to forgive, it helped me pray to forgive the man. I also prayed that I would not see other men as I saw him. As I prayed this prayer, I cried a lot but I don't know why. I wanted to sob from deep down inside but it wouldn't come up.

Rita's Notes. I stressed the importance of being in a good church fellowship and encouraged her to try a different one, since she wasn't happy where she had been going. When her self-image is especially low, she turns off the very people she likes by being too much in an infant role.

Creative Scene and Scripture

Beth's Journal. When we prayed, I saw an old rocking chair on a porch, and Jesus was sitting in it, and I was on His knee. I started to cry and said I didn't want to live. Rita said to tell Jesus that, and I did. Jesus told me I had to stay because He had work for me to do. Rita and Janet asked me if I was willing to do what Jesus wanted. I said I wanted to please Him but I didn't want to stay on earth. We prayed that I would be willing to be made willing.

Janet said, "Scripture teaches that God has opened a door for you and no one can shut it." I guess that means He has opened the door of my entrance into salvation when God came to live in me. I know this is true. But she also said, "And when God shuts a door, no one can open it and that includes you!" The door out of this life into the next and into the fullness of salvation can only be opened by the Lord (Revelation 3:7).[8] This was helpful because inside I was afraid I might try to "open the door."

[God used this word to Beth to give her God's inner controls when her own were weak.]

Rita's Notes. Next Beth shared with us some feelings she'd stuffed inside and never had expressed before. In her early teens she began to be normally attracted to the opposite sex. She didn't know what to do with these feelings, and thinking they were bad, she repressed them. (Here's where communication between mother and daughter would have helped.) In praying, Beth realized that because she didn't know how to cope with these emotions, she had not wanted to grow up and face them, and had drawn back into the safe role of an infant.

In her own words she says, "I think it caused me to repress the adult Beth and to allow only the little Beth to appear."

We explained to Beth, "God gave you the potential to have sexual feelings. They are a normal part of living. God intends your sexuality to come to full bloom in marriage. Having sexual feelings is not sin. What you do with those feelings, however, can be."

I like what a friend of mine, Joy Keyes, told me. She was counseling a person who had been sexually active before marriage and who had tried to curb these emotions after giving Jesus Lordship in her life. Joy's advice to her was, "When you feel these desires, thank God for them. Then put them in your personal bank account to be accumulated for the person God has for you, and the one you're to spend them on."

Today was another breakthrough for Beth, and we prayed further about this matter in February. Much more healing was still needed as the poem she wrote a short time later shows.

A SELF-PORTRAIT
(Beth's Journal—March 14, 1982)

"Who will love me?"
"No one, no one,
You are alone, alone,
Alone."

"Who will love me?"
"Nothing, nothing,
You are not worthy, worthy,
Worthy."

"Who will love me?"
Again she cries.
But this time
There is no reply.

No one, nothing,
Alone and unworthy.
Why live?
And thus she dies.

She explains in her journal, "This describes exactly how I feel right now. School pressures are heavy, and I don't like where I'm living. These things make me feel hopeless."

While these words may seem discouraging after reading about a number of significant healings, it shows the depth of Beth's need. Her "Self-Portrait" reveals that if she hadn't been actively seeking help, the outcome could have been serious.

Meanwhile, at the same time, Beth's *"New* Self-Portrait" was being painted stroke by stroke on God's canvas. It would soon emerge for others to see, but that's a further story. . . .

Reflection for Soul and Spirit

When you became a new creation in Christ, your spirit was joined to God and both spirit and soul were redeemed. Your spirit is a place of safety where God's Spirit dwells within you. The fruit and gifts of the Spirit, and God's rest and peace, dwell there. It is a most holy place within.

Your soul, or psychological nature, is a mixture of healed and unhealed emotions and memories; therefore, you cannot trust it to guide you. There may be areas that are still in rebellion to God. So you *must be* led by the Holy Spirit working through your spirit, and then out through the healed areas of your soul. You need to know the difference between your soul and your spirit.

1. What has the damaged, still-unhealed part of your soul been saying to you about yourself lately?
   Have you been agreeing with it?
   Frequently? Occasionally?

2. God told Beth she was special to Him. This new picture was hard for her to accept. What affirming words has God spoken to you?
   Have you been agreeing with Him?
   Will you try to distinguish between your soul and spirit and agree with God?

"The word of God [speaking of Jesus Himself, and also the Scripture) is quick, and powerful, and sharper than any twoedged sword, piercing even to the dividing asunder [cutting between] of soul and spirit . . ." Hebrews 4:12 KJV.

Prayer: Dear God, help me choose to believe what *You* say about me. Thank You that when I do this I choose to be on the winning side!

Chapter Seven

Beth Makes Peace
(Part Two)

A VERY SPECIAL FRIEND

He brought you into my life,
Just when I wanted to end it all.
Your bright, smiling eyes,
Penetrated me with God's love for me.
You are truly a saint of God,
Brightening my darkest days with love and understanding.

When God made you,
He took a piece of the sun to give you a glow in your eyes,
And He also gave you the Son's warm, loving arms
To hold and care for His little lost sheep.

My special friend,
When you were made God looked down from heaven,
Smiled and said,
"This little one will bring
love,
joy,
and peace,
to all the lives she touches!"

REBECCA BATTLE
(Galatians 5:22)

...Ye shall go out with joy,
And be led forth with peace:
The mountains and the hills
Shall break forth before you into singing,
And all the trees of the field
Shall clap their hands.

Isaiah 55:12 KJV

Y ou may be wondering about Beth's need to be held. You may ask if that's just her particular "thing."

Let me tell you a story. A year ago Dennis and I were in Orchard Park, New York, and were having dinner with the Reverend Tom Reid and his wife following a seminar at their church. A college professor who speaks extensively on the subject of love came into our conversation. The waitress overheard our discussion and told us, "The professor you're referring to is here in town; in fact, I heard him speak last night." She said, "At the end of his talk he told the audience if anyone wanted a hug, he would be available. The lineup was so long, it took him *two hours* to get through hugging people!" When I heard this, I wondered if churches offered more "hugs," whether there would be longer lines at their doors!

Iris Beardemphl, a Roman Catholic lay eucharistic minister, told us of an experience that happened to her during her weekly visit to a convalescent home for the elderly. The nurses told her which people would like her to visit them and pray with them. "There's a ninety-four-year-old woman here," they said, "whom we can't get through to at all. About the only communication we get from her is that numerous times during the day and night she yells, 'Help. I'm dying!' She's done this consistently over the last two years."

One day as Iris was nearby, sure enough the elderly woman yelled for help. Iris went into her room and asked, "How can I help you?"

The woman screamed, "Love me!" As Iris reached down and hugged her, the woman yelled, "Tighter, tighter!" Realizing the woman needed more than a brief hug, Iris lifted her fragile body from the wheelchair where she sat, carried her over to an easy chair, and held her on her lap as she would hold a baby. You can imagine what a long hug that woman needed! In fact, Iris continued to hold and hug her twenty minutes each week for the next eight months, until the woman's death. The hugging actually brought her out of senility, and she shared her whole life story with Iris.

The elderly woman had been like a drowning person yelling for help, but no one had known how to rescue her. There are a lot of people in this world yelling "Help" in various ways. But it takes the Holy Spirit's leading, as it did with Iris, to discover their needs and to find out how to meet them.

The Need to Be Held

The need to be held is universal. Being physically held and caressed was the basic way you received love (or should have received love) as a baby. A baby doesn't know enough language to receive love intellectually. If you had an adequate amount of holding in your infancy and childhood, you will feel satisfied. But if you, like Beth, did not have enough, you will crave it, daydream about it, and figure out numerous ways to get it. Many young people who are thought promiscuous are simply trying to get the hugs they never received. Other people, unfortunately, take advantage of their need.

There are accounts which show infants have actually died for lack of touch and loving attention. If you didn't get enough cuddling and holding in infancy and childhood, your feeling of self-worth will be weakened. But God created you, understands you, and has the answer when things haven't gone the way He intended for you.

God can transcend the natural with the supernatural. Through prayer He can give you, man or woman, the love you didn't receive. You don't have to wait in line two hours to receive a hug from Jesus! By the Holy Spirit, He can be "hugging" a whole room full of people at the same moment, and for as long as they need. He does often, however, use human channels to work through to help bring His love to people.

The second part of Beth's story will show you again how God's supernatural *agape* love bridges the gap between the love a child needed and the love parents were able to give.

Prenatal and Natal Prayer

April 20, 1982 (Beth's Journal). Today I saw that in compulsively looking for an older woman friend to hold me, I am looking for the ideal, loving mother I didn't feel I had. As this deep need is met through prayer, my need for holding will become normal.

We prayed prenatal prayer and release from effect of my mother's smoking, which cut into my oxygen supply, and also the effect of being born with the umbilical cord about my neck. We realized in prayer that these experiences prenatally and at birth carried over to my not feeling loved and accepted at birth. I felt that my mother didn't want to hold me when I was born. Perhaps she was afraid because I was so fragile. I forgave her for smoking and cutting my supply of oxygen.[1] I forgave her if in some way I had blamed her for the cord being wrapped around my neck. An infant wouldn't understand the reason for the choking feeling, and where it came from.

I asked God to forgive me for my reaction to these hurts connected with my mother, and asked God's forgiveness for hating my mother. I realized I hated my mother because I thought she didn't love me. I spoke forgiveness to my mother from the time of this past memory and asked God's forgiveness for my wrong attitude toward her.

Creative Prayer. We prayed a creative prayer and asked Jesus to allow me to see how He meant my mother to be.

First, Jesus held me really close, and I could feel His love. Then He handed me to my mother, and she showered my face with kisses. I really liked this. Then she touched my hands, and I wrapped my little fingers around her finger. Then she unwrapped my blanket and touched my legs and feet, and stroked me all over. My mother then nursed me. I didn't want to stop nursing but I was getting too full. Janet said the supply would be there whenever I wanted it; I didn't have to take it all right now. I could have more when I wanted it. I was really glad she said that because I couldn't stop drinking, but I felt physically uncomfortable because I was so full.

My mother continued to hold me close. I dozed off and on for quite a while. Then Jesus picked me up, held me, and carried me back to the nursery.

I noticed the *nursing desire* had the same feeling the *holding desire* has. I felt ashamed that I want nursing so much. As healing was taking place with my mother, I leaned toward Janet for comfort, but the creative prayer stopped when I did this. I realized I couldn't go to others for the love I needed from my mother.

April 23, 1982. For a few days after I could feel my mother still holding and touching me, but I couldn't see her face. Then I couldn't see the picture at all. I tried to picture the nursing scene but I couldn't, even though I wanted to very much.

Here you see the importance of the leading of the Holy Spirit. There was nothing wrong with Beth's desire to relive something good, but it had to be according to God's timing and direction. You can see once again that soul-healing prayer is not an intellectual exercise but the therapeutic work of the Lord.

End of the School Year

June 3, 1982 (Rita's Notes). Beth was exhausted because she had worked so hard to make perfect grades. Even though she did make excellent grades, she still saw herself as a failure, and felt lonely. The feeling of "not making it" had returned, plus her often-repeated syndrome of looking for a mother figure had again caused a conflict with a person at college. She felt "bad" because her desire to be held was strong again.

This didn't surprise me. I've learned in praying for others who were very wounded that healing is a process. Much progress will be made, and then a problem on the job or in a relationship, for example, will set the person back a few steps. It's important to know that he or she won't fall all the way back to ground zero, provided some healing of emotions and memories has already taken place. A support system of those who can love and pray for him or her is very important.

Beth was also worried about her friendship with her new friend, Karen, yet another mother figure. Because of her need for love and attention, she was getting too dependent and already beginning to strain the friendship.

Today she felt that no one, not even the Lord, loved her. We suggested she ask Him if that was true, and she said she felt she got a "yes." I assured her that He *does* love her, but sometimes we have to simply trust He does even when our emotions feel to the contrary. Then she said that we, her prayer-counselors, didn't love her. We asked if she really believed that after all the time we'd been together. Finally she admitted, "Yes, I believe you love me, Rita and Janet, but it's hard for me to say this because I'm afraid the moment I say it, you'll stop. It seems when I confess something good it stops happening."

Creative Prayer. We prayed about Beth's loneliness. She saw herself in a garden. She said she couldn't see or feel Jesus there with her and that worried her.

I said, "Beth, in the Book of Romans, Saint Paul says no one can separate a believer from the love of God. He said 'For I am persuaded that neither death nor life, nor angels nor principalities nor powers, nor things present nor things to come, nor height nor depth, nor any other created thing, shall be able to separate us from the love of God which is in Christ Jesus our Lord.' (Romans 8:38, 39).

"There's only one person who can separate you from God, and that's you yourself. Sin can separate you from God, but your erroneous feeling that you are bad or unworthy can do it also. What," I asked, "do you think could be causing your feeling of separation?"

Beth thought a moment and responded, "It could be that I'm idolizing women and not putting Jesus first." With that she asked God's forgiveness, cast away a spirit of idolatry, and asked God to cleanse and fill her. After this she was able to see Jesus with her, as they walked in the garden together.

We thought of the old gospel song "In the Garden," and we repeated the words as Beth pictured herself there with Jesus. The words tell very well what is experienced in soul-healing prayer. Read it slowly to yourself, and see what I mean.

I come to the garden alone,
while the dew is still on the roses;
And the voice I hear,
falling on my ear,
the Son of God discloses.

And He walks with me,
and He talks with me,
And He tells me I am His own,
And the joy we share as we tarry there,
None other has ever known."

C. AUSTIN MILES

Needing to Grow Up

Beth's Journal. Rita, Janet, and I prayed about my fears of being unsuccessful and "not making it." I found it really hard to pray this as I'm still afraid of responsibility and having to grow up. When I have tried to be responsible, it has become a burden, and after a while I can't handle it. I began by asking Jesus to make me willing to grow up.

Prayer for Infancy

July 12, 1982 (Rita's Notes). Because of the connection between Beth's need for excessive holding and her unfulfilled need to be close to her mother in infancy, it seemed a good idea to pray further about her nursing period. She had tried to pray about this by herself but couldn't. I suggested she put her head on Janet's shoulder, and we would pray and ask the Holy Spirit to lead.

Beth could then see herself nursing with her mother. All went well with the prayer until we came to the point where she was six months old, and then the nursing seemed to stop. This puzzled us until we realized that when she was six months old her mother became pregnant again, and Beth's nursing at her mother's breast had to stop.[2]

Beth told us she had begun sucking her thumb at this point. It became a real problem and she eventually had to wear braces to correct buck teeth.

Beth had a number of people to forgive. She forgave her father for getting her mother pregnant so soon; forgave her mother for conveying the feeling of rejection; and forgave her sister for her existence. Finally, Beth asked God to forgive her for where she had been wrong.

Beth's Journal. We prayed about the time when my mother and baby sister came home from the hospital. [Jesus was there to hold me, a fourteen-month-old infant, so I wouldn't feel alone.] [A month later] My mom is with my sister and I'm standing away from them feeling rejected and lonely. Next I see myself in my sister's room and I take her bottle. At the time it happened, I was punished.

This time, with Jesus there, my mom bends down, picks me up, and says to me, "You really like that bottle don't you? Let's go and get you one of your own." I could feel her love and understanding just like I do with Rita and Janet. I then forgave my mom, from my child-self.

We prayed about the hospital scene again. Beth said she still felt angry about this memory and realized that she had an irrational anger against her mother as though *she* was the one who had caused her to go to the hospital.

Rita's Notes. We guided Beth to ask the Lord's forgiveness for blaming her mother for her needing the surgery. She thanked God that her mother recognized she needed treatment, and for saving her life by taking her to the hospital. Beth's friend Karen, who had joined us for our prayer session, moved easily in soul-healing prayer.

July 14, 1982. Two Days Later. Beth said, "I have continued to see the creative scene with my mother, me, and the bottle, and I do feel understood by her. This is something I have *never* felt before in my life."

Desire to Obey God

August 17, 1982 (Rita's Notes). Beth has regressed heavily since our last visit. We discovered later that she was actually recovering from a near-breakdown from all the stress at the university. She had felt she had to make *A*s, and with the emotional battles going on inside, she had had to study longer hours and had pushed herself to the breaking point.

As our session began she started talking about her desire to be held. This was causing problems with Karen. I asked, "Do you want to be a child or an adult?" She answered, "An adult, but I still want to be held." Beth put her head on my shoulder, I put my arm around her and began to pray.

She realized this time that what I was praying about was blocked out so that she couldn't even hear it, due to the fact that she was being held at the same time. She told us that Jesus spoke to her in a firm voice and told her to "sit up." Her fear of disobeying God was greater than her desire to be held.

[I've found that, after you've begun to be healed, God will eventually draw you up short when you try to revert into old habit patterns and escape mechanisms. This is what He was doing with Beth. God wanted her to know she was more healed than she realized.]

Deliverance Prayer

Beth thought she might be needing specific deliverance. Janet and I asked her to name the wrong spirits she felt were oppressing her. After claiming the protection of the blood of Jesus over us all, we had her name the wrong spirits and follow with, "I bind you under the blood of Jesus. I render you powerless in my life and I cast you out, in Jesus' name." We prayed against spirits of false guilt, self-pity, lust of the flesh, destruction, rejection, inordinate affection, confusion, rebellion, compulsion, wrong fantasy, and "a counterfeit will that tries to be God in my life." Then we asked the Holy Spirit to fill Beth.

One needs to use deliverance prayers cautiously with a very wounded person. Her self-identity is so damaged that you should be sure to tell her that though her soul needs deliverance, her spirit is secure in Jesus. You must be sure she (or he) is ready and willing to pray for deliverance. In all these ways it was the right time for Beth.

When we finished praying I asked, "Beth, did you feel anything in particular during these prayers?"

She answered, "Yes, the deliverance prayer about the will made me realize my mother crushed my will when I was ten by paddling me until I finally gave up." Here's her account of our prayer together:

Beth's Journal (Reliving—Creative Prayer). Jesus showed me the scene where my mother was spanking me really hard. As she spanked me she looked at me with hatred; when I responded with hatred in my eyes she kept spanking me until I stopped.

I saw my will lying on the floor like a limp dishrag. I thought it was dead. Rita asked me to pick it up and give it to Jesus. Jesus took it and molded it like it was clay. I saw Him make one long large ridge in it, then He put a little light, like a candle flame, in it. He gently put it inside me without hurting me. He said, "The flame will grow."

We thought of the song "Have Thine Own Way" and, holding hands, we sang the first verse together:

> *Have Thine own way, Lord!/Have Thine own way!*
> *Thou art the Potter;/I am the clay!*
> *Mold me and make me/After Thy will,*
> *While I am waiting,/Yielded and still.*
>
> ADELAIDE POLLARD

Another breakthrough! Beth's crushed will was healed and now she would have more strength in making decisions and overcoming extreme passivity.

Beth's Journal (Creative Prayer). We prayed a creative prayer where Jesus had a talk with my mother about her treatment of me. When He was finished, my mother was crying, and she told me she was sorry. That was the first time my mother ever apologized to me. Next I forgave my mother and asked Jesus to help her know His love.

Rita's Notes. We discussed the possibility that Beth's inordinate need for hugging was a way of trying to absorb by osmosis the attributes of an admired person into herself. We discussed unacceptable and acceptable ways to handle her desire for holding:

1. She could continue letting the Hurt Little Child stay in control, eventually causing people she cares for to reject her.

2. She could sublimate the desire by other activities. (This is good but it doesn't get rid of the desire, which is always in back of the mind, unsatisifed.)

3. She could get physical affirmation from her friends during soul-healing prayer. We normally begin and close our sessions with hugs, and give them at other times during prayer when they seem to be needed. (This helps for a time but is not a total answer.)

4. She could experience Jesus' love during soul-healing prayer and let Him hold her and show her how He had intended her parents to love her. (This is truly healing.)

5. She could pass on the love she received to others who need healing. (An ultimate goal.)

6. Someday she might marry, and so express her love in another adult way.

God's Affirmation

We prayed for the Lord to show Beth her attributes as a woman.

Instead of seeing herself as an adult, she saw herself at the age of three sitting on Jesus' knee, and asked Him, "Will you show me my attributes as a woman?" What He said didn't make sense to Beth, and at first she didn't want to tell us. We encouraged her to share it anyway.

Beth said, "He said I'm obedient," but I'm not! Janet replied, "But that's how *God* sees you because He knows that's the desire of your heart; also it could be a look into the future of your life."

Beth said shyly, "He also told me that I'm gentle and kind."

We thanked God for affirming His child. We also realized that these are three of the attributes of Jesus. He is of all people obedient, gentle, and kind.

Beth's new friend, Karen, was truly sent by the Lord. Beth needed less time for prayer and personal affirmation from us now that she had the support of someone nearby, and she found that she would soon need that support.

That fall she phoned telling us that the sponsoring teacher for her internship was making it very difficult. Beth was required to teach yoga, and let it be known that it was against her religious beliefs. The teacher was quite annoyed. She didn't seem to like Beth, criticizing her many times a day. Even though Beth had made an *A* average the previous semester, thereby receiving a scholarship for her internship, she saw no other way to work it out other than choosing voluntary withdrawal near the end of that semester.

She returned to her job working with handicapped children, and with the pressure off, things went along better. We didn't want to stop praying with Beth until she was strong enough to stand on her own, but Janet and I felt she had already come a long way. Meantime, Dennis's and my travel schedule continued to increase. Janet and I didn't pray with Beth at all in 1983.

Beth kept in touch with us through letters and phone calls, but they were friendly contacts, rather than calls from need.

Dennis and I visited Beth when our travels took us down to her location. We were disappointed her educational pursuits had been stopped, and glad when she found new direction. She decided to take some time off from college, and later, work for a degree which would allow her to teach preschool children. She could take those future studies at a slower pace, while continuing to work.

Over the phone Beth and I talked about her old prose poem, rewriting it now from a healed outlook.

A NEW PORTRAIT

"Who will love me?"
Jesus, Rita, Janet, Karen
I am not alone, alone,
alone.

"Who will love me?"
Oh, so many friends!
I am now worthy, worthy,
Worthy."

"Who will love me?"
Again she cries,
But this time
Such a different reply.

"God loves me!"
My friends, and parents love me.
I'm not alone
or unworthy.

"Why live?"
Comes a further reply.
"To share God's love and life,
So others need not die."

The Final Key

A year had gone by when Beth came up to the Seattle area again. In the meantime she had been praying with Karen and Karen's husband, and realized that she had a repressed hatred for men. She had intended the present trip as just a friendly visit with Janet, but after Beth shared her new insight, they decided to pray. I was not with them, due to my traveling schedule. I had reluctantly asked Janet to choose a new prayer partner, which she was in the process of doing. Janet began now to write up the prayer sessions, as I had done, and Beth continued to keep her journal.

September 9, 1984 (Janet's Notes). Beth met with me for the first time after many months. It was well over a year and the first time without Rita being there also. Beth felt she knew what we were to pray about, but had been fearful to explore it alone. She said inner healing was the only thing that had really helped her ... not counseling, not psychotherapy, not even church. So we began to pray and let the Holy Spirit lead.

Beth's Journal. Janet prayed for me and asked if Jesus was with me. I said, "yes." Then I felt myself in a very dark room and I was really scared. I was two or three years old. I prayed for Jesus to be close beside me, which helped, but I was still afraid. Then I knew why.

There was a man [perhaps a teenager] in the room, and he wanted to hurt me. He hurt me (molested me sexually). Jesus then came actively into the scene and talked to the man (Jesus was angry with him) and sent him away.

Jesus came to me, quieted me down, and healed me. He picked me up and told me *I was not dirty or bad.* After Jesus told me this I felt clean and light.

The scene of my attacker reappeared to me, and Janet asked if I could see Jesus there. I could, and Jesus stood between me and the man. Jesus sent the man away again. Jesus told me He would protect me from further harm. This scene tried to reappear quite a few times, but each time it does, I just see Jesus standing between me and the man, and it goes away.

After this memory was healed, Jesus and I were in a meadow full of wild flowers. I would run up to Jesus, He would catch me up in His arms, and then throw me in the air and catch me. After a time of healthy childhood fun, I prayed forgiveness for the man and that he would find Jesus.

I asked the Lord, "Is this the reason for my fear of men's sexuality?" And He said, "Partly." Although I don't want to know who the man was at this point, I am curious to know where the scene took place, whether at home with a baby-sitter, or during my long stay at the hospital. I feel the results of this prayer time will bring a lot of healing and growth.

Self-Evaluation

Beth's Journal. I feel Jesus is healing me.

1. Usually when I return from seeing Rita and Janet, I go through a week or two of missing them terribly and wanting holding. This time I didn't experience this. *Maybe I don't need holding as much now.*
2. *I feel that the little girl has begun to grow up.* She is no longer a baby but a little girl about four or five years old. I know this is not a great jump, but after years of being between one and three it is indeed progress!

It's clear to see that the childhood sexual abuse caused Beth to stop maturing emotionally; now she could begin to grow up.

I believe this was the root cause for Beth's irrational feeling of being "bad." This root was unknown until it was revealed and removed by the Holy Spirit. The other experiences that followed her in life had built upon this unrevealed foundation. Her mother, her father, and others unknowingly built on it until the attitude of being a "bad" person was fully ingrained in her personality.

That October Beth and Janet prayed about the memory of child molestation again, and got out some repressed anger toward her parents for not protecting her. She was angry at her mother for not knowing what had happened and for not comforting her. (This is speaking from the child's viewpoint.) They had a creative, reconciling prayer about her parents.

Prayer time finished, Janet and Beth discussed inviting her parents to stay with her at her home when they came to visit. She prayed for Jesus to change her feelings so she would want to have them with her. This was another forward step.

Later that year, Beth told us that she had invited her parents to her home. While she and her mother were sitting on the couch talking, her mother reached over and put her arm around her and held her. It felt good, and she could receive it. She had never before remembered a time when her mother had given her that kind of physical tenderness and love. So, as with Beth's classmate at college several years before, the healing that was first experienced during soul-healing prayer later took place in life.

Janet asked Marilyn, another experienced prayer-counselor, to join her and they met with Beth four times in 1985. Several things stand out in their accounts.

February and April 1985

Social Integration

Beth had an irrational fear of people she didn't know, on the job and in other places. The Lord showed that here, too, the root cause was the childhood molestation.

Satan enjoys causing people to have irrational fears and wants to separate them from others, just as a wolf enjoys separating one little sheep from the rest. As I've often seen, the enemy enjoys attacking a person's sexuality early in life, wounding them so far back that it's no longer consciously remembered, and therefore impossible to deal with unless with love and prayer it's allowed to surface.

Beth's mother also had a prejudice toward people she didn't know, and consequently negative feelings were built into Beth's foundation. These made it hard for Beth to socialize. She always felt she didn't "fit." As Beth, Janet and Marilyn prayed through these memories, Beth began to be more open.

August 24, 1985 (Beth's Journal—With Janet and Marilyn). We began talking about social problems, and how I feel I don't fit in or belong anywhere. Janet asked if I felt I fit in at school; I remembered the second grade as my worst year, and the sixth grade as the best.

She suggested we start at the sixth grade. I pictured it with pleasure. The teacher was never angry with me, and he was gentle and kind. He also asked me to help an older student whom no one got along with. My prayer-counselors suggested that when I was in an environment where I felt loved and accepted, I was free to be a happy, healthy person.

Next I pictured a scene in ninth grade where I admired and looked up to an older girl. I followed her around a lot, and finally she reported me to a counselor. The counselor phoned my mother and stated she felt I was homosexual. My teacher confronted me with the information. I couldn't respond or talk about it, but really felt bad because I didn't want to be homosexual (whatever that meant). At home, my mother gave me a book on the subject, and when I was alone in my room, I looked up what homosexual meant. I read and reread this information many times in the following years.

I forgave a lot of people today.

[Beth has never participated in homosexual activity.]

Cinderella Syndrome

November 1, 1985 (Beth's Journal—Creative Prayer). A scene came to memory when I was about twelve or thirteen [about a year younger than the preceding memory]. I was at home in the kitchen cooking dinner and cleaning the house. My mom and dad were outside having a party, and my sister and brother were playing. This was an often-repeated experience. I felt like Cinderella, and was very lonely. I realized Jesus was there and He helped me do the work (He did most of it).

When we were finished, Jesus said I could go outside and play. I took out my doll things and Jesus helped me carry them outside. Once set up, I played dolls by myself.

Soon my mother noticed I was outside, came over to me and started scolding me because I had finished the work too quickly and therefore couldn't have done a good job. I returned to the house feeling very sad and rejected, and that no one loved or wanted me. I started to cry because I wasn't allowed to be a little girl. I always seemed to have to be the adult. When my parents had a party, it was usually my job to help clean up afterwards, and then prepare dinner for the family.

Janet led me in prayer to forgive my mother for being unfair in demanding too much housework of me for my age, for her critical attitude and words, and for not giving me the loving care I needed.

Janet also told me, "Jesus loves you." But I said, "Jesus loves everyone." She then said, "You are special to Jesus. Can you hear Jesus talking to you?" I listened prayerfully and said, "Yes . . . Jesus told me that He's proud of me and that I have a good attitude in the midst of an unfair situation." This felt good to me but I still hurt inside, and the hurt was so big it wouldn't go away.

Janet asked, "Can you let Jesus touch you?" I couldn't because I didn't think He really wanted to. She talked to me some more and explained how in the Bible Jesus sometimes healed through touch. She assured me that He wanted to touch me and asked, "Can you see Him reaching out to you?" We waited and I saw Jesus reaching out to touch my head. When He touched me, I saw a sudden burst of light around and over my head and felt a tingling sensation go through my body to my arms and hands. *The hurt left at the same time!*

Then I saw myself as a child again. I sat in Jesus' lap and He comforted me. After quite a while of enjoying Jesus' love, they asked, "Is there anything more?" I said, "Yes, Jesus sent me out to play again. This time I've joined my friends who are playing in the street while Jesus is in the house making dinner."

Janet's Notes. It was interesting that before the healing, Beth went to play alone with her dolls, and after the healing she went to play with her peers.

I told her that her sixth grade was like a parable of her life. When she is in a healthy environment, free from condemnation and accepting herself as a lovable and capable person, she is free to relate to others with freedom. Also that she has been a friend to the friendless, but now can also be a friend to those who have friends. She prayed that she would not forget the friendless ones.

Beth feels so much better about herself. The following day at the church coffee hour, instead of keeping close beside me every moment, she mingled in the crowded room to get her coffee and doughnut. She wouldn't have been this free before Jesus healed the hurt with her mother. Thank You, Lord.

These were further breakthrough experiences. It had taken seven years for the ninth-grade memory of being labeled homosexual to come up in prayer. Beth's mother did her best to inform and help her daughter, but unintentionally confirmed the counselor's diagnosis. A mother's opinion on such a matter is like something written in wet cement in a child's heart. Once it has set, it is very hard to remove. Then her mother's attitude continued to push her away from the very loving attention she needed so she could grow up without hang-ups.

There was a cumulative effect in the prayers over the years, but being healed of the early childhood molestation followed by receiv-

ing Jesus' healing touch were the two crucial experiences that built
on all the others to restore her identity. The next time I talked to
Beth she told me, "Now when I pray, one small change makes a
big difference, whereas, at the beginning one large prayer made only
a dent in my needs." When the Lord's axe is laid to the root, the
bad tree cannot continue to exist (Matthew 3:10).

Cautions

It's important not to guess about something like early molestation. Janet had several indications before praying in this area. First,
Beth, the counselee, began to be led in that direction. Second, there
were clues such as a deep fear of unknown people, especially men.
Third, she had an irrational feeling of being "bad."

Don't try to dig into the person's subconscious memories for hidden data.
Pray about the memories which are already known, and as you go
along the Holy Spirit will reveal what is unknown, if needed, and
at the right time.

Don't tell a person what to see, hear, or feel. Trust that the Holy
Spirit will guide in all these ways. Don't try to do God's work for
Him. If you do, it won't be effective. If the Lord seems to give you
a word of knowledge or discernment, it should confirm what the
counselee feels God is saying.

For further direction and advice about prayer-counseling I refer
you to my previous books, and to other reliable books on the subject, which you will find listed in the bibliographies in this and my
other books.

The Fruit Shows

The day came when Beth phoned me to proclaim, *"I'm healed!"*
By the conviction in her voice and the witness in my own spirit, I
knew it was true! With a big smile on my face I said, "Tell me
about it."

Beth said, "I never say I want to die anymore. I really want to live. *I don't feel I'm 'bad' any more.* That completely left when the Lord healed me from the early childhood molestation memory. I still have some struggles but *nothing* like before. I used to hurt all the time, but now my healing is so established I even forget *how* I used to hurt. You know, Rita," she said, "if it hadn't been for that first prayer on the telephone, and all the prayers that followed, I wouldn't be alive. Now I have so much to live for!"

Here's a "before and after" healing list that Beth wrote in her journal concerning her parents:

Before: Loved and respected my parents because of God's commands.
After: Love and respect my parents by choice freely.

Before: Blamed my parents for not giving me what I needed to grow up healthy and happy.
After: Love my parents for doing the best they could for me.

Before: Would never tell my mother anything of a personal nature.
After: Beginning to really talk to my mother.

Beth is back in college just as she planned. Getting a teacher's certificate will help her achieve her dream to have a center for handicapped children, with a Christian emphasis.

Beth is still working on some areas in her life which need healing but she's living on a totally new level. She is giving as well as receiving with greater freedom. She has a new hairdo more in keeping with her age, she has lost weight, and dresses more in style. Best of all, she is a gentle, sensitive, caring person, and a joy to be around. She's experiencing the "peace that passes understanding" but also that passes on to others. That's what makes a difference in this world—people passing on the peace of God.

Fathers, too, can pass this peace along, as we'll see . . .

Soul-Healing Preparation, Reflection, and Creative Prayer

Preparation. Assuming that you've read Appendixes A and B, we can pray without further preparation. If you skipped over these steps please turn to the back of the book, and read these Appendixes.

You may have noticed that Beth was led by the Holy Spirit to pray creative prayers more frequently than some of the other kinds. Creative prayer is one effective way to allow God's joy and restoring power to work in your life. Some people find this way to pray easier than others do.

Since I can't work with you individually, directions for prayer will obviously not be as flexible as I would choose. Bear with me. I'll give you some ideas for ways to pray, and then you need to ask the Lord which would be best for you. Follow His leading.

When you experience or see the Lord in prayer, you are actually, as the Scripture says, "perceiving Him after the Spirit." You may not be able to describe Him to anyone else. That's not important. It's being aware of His Presence that's important. It's also important to learn to hear His voice. I'm not talking about hearing an audible voice, but that inner knowing in your spirit that He has spoken.

Reflection. We want to see Jesus, our resurrected Lord.

Mary Magdalene saw Him as an everyday sort of Person—a gardener.

Cleopas and his fellow disciple on the road to Emmaus didn't recognize Him at first either, but experienced Him as the Counselor who brought them out of depression.

The disciples in the Upper Room saw Him as the powerful Lord who walked through locked doors and then sat down and ate with them.

Paul saw Him in blinding light and was thrown to the ground by His Presence so He could "reason together" with him.

And John the Revelator saw Him a King in royal garments, with feet as brass refined by fire, and a voice like a waterfall.

All these pictures reveal to us what the Lord Jesus is like, but we know that each of us individually needs to see Jesus "after the Spirit"; He wants to show Himself to us for our own healing and life.[3] (*Pause here.*)

A Creative Prayer for You. Pray with me, "Lord, I cast down all vain or useless imaginations and every high thing that exalts itself against the knowledge of God. Through You, Lord Jesus, I pull down strongholds and bring into captivity every thought to the obedience of Christ. In all my ways I acknowledge You so You can direct my pathway. (Personalized from 2 Corinthians 10:5 and Proverbs 3:6.)

"Thank You, Lord, for giving me a vision of Yourself so that I won't perish from thirst in this dusty old world. Thank You that as I behold Your face 'as in a glass' I am changed to be like You—'beholding You I am made whole.' Thank You that Your Word says to seek Your face, Your Presence, continually. Teach me how to do this. Through sin and hurts I've lost creativity; forgive me and heal me so that I can see with spiritual eyes. Heal my oldness and renew my childlike wonder. 'Open our eyes Lord, we want to see Jesus'. Amen."[4] (*Take some time here to enjoy the Lord's loving Presence.*)

Now let Him do for you what you needed most in your childhood. He wants to give to you even more than you want to receive.

Did you need to be held?

Were you lonely?

Did you need a dad to play ball or some other game?

Did you need someone to help you deliver papers, take a walk with, play dolls with, or any number of things?

Did you need someone to help you study?

Did you need someone to celebrate your birthday?

Let Jesus meet you at your point of need. In the Scripture He usually asked people: "What do you want me to do for you?" (Mark 10:51 NIV). He's asking you that question too. (*Take some time here and tell the Lord what you need.*)

"Dear Lord, thank You for meeting me at my place of need. I know You want to bring peace to my life; please bring deep peace and rest on every level. You are the Prince of Peace. Thank You for doing for me what no one else can. Thank You, Lord."

(*Put this book aside for now, and wait in the Lord's Presence to receive from Him.*)

Chapter Eight

Peace With Your Father

And the peace of God, which passes all understanding,
will keep your hearts and your minds in Christ Jesus.
Philippians 4:7 RSV

Let the peace of Christ rule in your hearts,
Since as members of one body;
You were called to peace.
And be thankful.

Colossians 3:15 NIV

Unless you forgive your father, you may spend a lifetime drawing to yourself and battling angrily those men (and sometimes women) who remind you of your father. (This is also true about mothers.)

God has given me numerous opportunities to see this. I am a former child-welfare social worker. I've been a minister's wife for more than twenty years; a speaker and teacher in Christian work for twenty-five; and I've worked specifically in soul-healing prayer since 1978. You can imagine I've had opportunities to talk with thousands of hurting women and men!

At times I get letters like this:

> I feel the Lord has told me I have to forgive my parents, and love them, but I just can't! My parents don't live far from me; however, I never want to go home. I can't stand being in the same room with them for more than half an hour!

The writer of that letter is right when he says that in order to walk in peace with God and man, you must forgive your parents. But God doesn't only say "you must," He wants to show you *how*. Some believe all that is needed to effect change is to confront the person with what he has done wrong and what the Bible says he should do, but this can just add to the guilt unless he is helped to do it. The Gospel message is not "try harder," but "Jesus saves." He came to change us, to give us the power to live the way He wants us to. Through prayer you can allow Jesus to heal your hurts so that you are able to forgive.

Some Basic Categories of Need

The problems children have with fathers are various:

> There are fathers who divorce their wives without any effort at reconciliation with their children, leaving the children feeling abandoned.

> There are alcoholic fathers who cause embarrassment and hurt because they are often physically and emotionally absent, and because of their erratic, sometimes angry and violent behavior.

> There are strict authoritarian fathers who maintain strong discipline but give little physical affection and love to their family.

> There are fathers who don't accept their children's sexual identity. For example, insisting that a daughter fill the role of

a son, to meet the father's own need for fulfillment; or simply rejecting the child for being born the "wrong" sex.

There are controlling fathers who don't allow their children to grow up.

There are weak-willed fathers who can't stand up to domineering mothers.

There are fathers who never affirm their sons and daughters. They give them no praise, and don't recognize their achievements.

There are fathers who abuse their children, either verbally, physically, or sexually.

This listing is not given to blame anyone, but to help you determine where your needs might be. There are no perfect parents, just as there are no perfect children. We don't, however, have to keep passing on weaknesses from one generation to another. If parents would seek their own wholeness, they could pass it on to their children, and the vicious cycle would be broken.

Fathering Is Important

Why should we be so concerned about bridging the father gap? Leanne Payne puts it this way, "Whether we are men or women, it is to the masculine we must look for the strong, fatherly affirmation of our sexual identity and of ourselves as persons."[1] At puberty and adolescence following, the affirming and loving presence of the father is critical to a son's or daughter's self-esteem. An accepting father validates a son's masculinity and a daughter's femininity. This means the father must make himself available to his children.

A little girl gets her primary sexual identity from her mother, and the boy gets his from his father, but evidently it's important for both sons and daughters to have their fathers affirm them and accept their identity.

In our American culture, fathers have often taken a backseat in the lives of their children, and it's true in some other cultures too. I believe the trend is changing for us. Realizing how important it is, many fathers are taking an active part at the beginning of their children's lives, even to being present at birth itself, for early bonding. Men are helping more with early child-raising, not waiting for the kids to be "dry at both ends" before paying real attention to them! As Jesus did, they are allowing the little children to come to them.

A Balance in Showing Love

A normal part of growing up for a daughter is to "fall in love" with her daddy. After she goes through this phase, she begins to relate to mother again, this time in a closer and more mature way, and begins to pattern after her mother. During these times of preference, the parents need to guard against being jealous and competing for the daughter's attention, so as not to confuse the growth process she's going through.

(The boy goes through a similar phase in reverse with his mother and father, as I mentioned in chapter 5, and then should develop a mature relationship with his father. Again parents should guard against competition.)

If a father has serious, unhealed hurts in his own life, and doesn't understand the phase of growth his daughter is passing through and her need to try out her feminine charm on him, he may be tempted to take advantage of her. If he does so, he will wound her deeply, and do harm that would be irreparable were it not for the healing power of God.

I've prayed with scores of women who in childhood and youth were abused sexually by their fathers. In Diana Russell's research paper to which I referred in chapter 4, she reports that out of 930 women studied, 16 percent had suffered some kind of sexual abuse from a close relative, and 4 percent of these were abused by their fathers. One in five who were raised by a stepfather had been abused by him. Significantly, the educational and social level of the families made no difference to the statistics. "Daughters of doctors and college professors were as likely to be abused as were the daughters of blue-collar workers."

Each woman I have prayed with has been healed, but for years they had lived with unhealed hurts that often prevented a wholesome relationship with men.

There can also be overcorrection in the opposite direction. A father may be fearful of giving his daughter *any* physical love at all, lest he create a problem. Father John Hampsch, a Roman Catholic Claretian Priest, tell us that girls ages seven to eleven, who are deprived of a father's love, are later unable to respond fully to a husband's love. They may actually become deficient intellectually. He says there's no cure for this condition other than God's cure.[2] Those in counseling fields say in some instances even a girl's physical maturation can be arrested by her father's failing to express his affection.

Father and author, Gary Smalley says, "Touch deprivation can leave a daughter with deep-seated feelings of unacceptance."[3]

So father, do whatever you can to successfully bring your daughter through this stage of seeking to be specially close to you. You'll be able to tell when the reservoir of father's love has been filled, because her need will diminish.

When expressing affection to your daughter, here are a few guidelines:

1. *For special times of physical contact and holding, make it a policy to have mother there with you.* For example, you and your wife and the children can have times when you all pile on the couch, arms around one another, and read favorite books together.

2. *It's wiser to kiss your daughter on the cheek, rather than on the mouth.* If you do kiss her on the lips, let it only be a loving "peck"!

3. *If your daughter wears clothes that are too brief and too revealing, talk it over with your wife.* This will be a good opportunity for her to teach the daughter modesty, and help her understand that God created the male to be stimulated by seeing the female figure; just as in contrast, the woman is stimulated by loving things the man says to her. Dressing in good taste is for her own protection regardless of what the modern trend may be. (Be reasonable! I'm not speaking of high-neck dresses with long sleeves!)

4. *If you sense in yourself an abnormal physical attraction to your daughter during times of closeness, it may indicate you need to pray for soul healing.* Sometimes it's simply a matter of "Casting down imaginations . . . and bringing into captivity every thought to the obedience of Christ" (2 Corinthians 10:5 KJV). Or it may indicate needs in you that are unmet. You, and very likely your wife, too, may need to seek help through inner healing or from a Christian marriage counselor.

If the mother is divorced or widowed, she should try her best to keep a positive male presence in her children's lives. In the case of divorce, she should encourage the father to spend time with his children. If he is not a good influence, or if the father has died, there are other males who can bridge the gap. Grandfathers, brothers, stepfathers, uncles, godparents, or friends who are willing to be surrogate parents; one of these can help fill the vacancy, and give your children the affirmation they need. If the father substitute is married, his wife must be willing to be a part of the process. The same cautions I just listed for you apply for him as for the natural father. (You may need to seek advice from your pastor on these matters.)

Many men and women are immature, and some are in identity crises, because they have missed out on these early steps in their normal process of growth and development.

My Father

Attempting to be transparent, I've told you something about my relationship with my mother. You may have wondered about my father. I had a good father. William Harvey Reed, now with the Lord, was a good-living man. He didn't waste money on bad habits, tell off-color jokes or use profanity. He did not physically abuse his children but provided for them the best he could.

He was a Christian. Raised in the Presbyterian church, he met the Lord personally during his early years.

My father was ahead of his time in that he was present and assisting by giving ether at the birth of his first two children, both born at home. Dad had learned to administer anesthesia on the front lines in an ambulance company during World War I. His grandfather had been a surgeon. When my dad was fifteen, his father gave him the key to his grandfather's medical library, because he was interested in medicine and liked to read; he spent a lot of time there. As part of his wartime duty he volunteered to assist the surgeons with amputations and other emergencies on the field of battle.

My father wasn't present at the births of my older sister and me. We were born in the hospital, and fathers weren't normally allowed in the delivery room in those days, as they are today. So we missed out on this special experience of immediate bonding with our father which people are only now beginning to realize is important.

Dad always loved little children. If he passed a child when walking along the sidewalk, or in a store, he would usually say hello. If appropriate, he would pat the child on the head.

I always enjoyed my dad in childhood. He had a big deep voice, and I liked to hear it as he talked or read the newspaper aloud to my mother.

Because of the move to Florida, from age two to three and a half I saw my dad only when he came down for Christmas, until he finally succeeded in selling his business in Michigan and could join us. Many early hurts that are barely if at all consciously remembered occur around ages two to three, and that would have been an important time for me to have been with my dad.

From Law to Grace

Our religious experiences as a family were both good and bad. Good, because in my childhood I received the most wonderful gift of all, Jesus Christ. I also learned about the power of the Holy Spirit. Bad, because the legalistic rules insisted upon were far too rigid and took away a lot of the fun we should have enjoyed as we grew up. I chafed under such restrictions as "no lipstick, no ballet lessons, no movies, no games with playing cards" which created needless conflict.

Someone said, "If you were raised under 'law' you'll probably need more inner-healing prayer than if you were raised under 'grace.' "

Something had happened just a month before my father's graduation from high school that must have affected him deeply and damaged his feeling of self-worth. He and his next older brother got into an argument over walking some girls home from a band concert. There were words and a bit of roughhousing. His father, my grandfather, was a strict disciplinarian and told my dad he would have to leave, and begin to make his own way in the world. So the very next morning my father, at the age of seventeen, with ten dollars in his pocket (worth a lot more than today, of course), climbed on a train for the big city of Detroit. By God's grace and his own perseverance he did find a job, and eventually found my mother, too, working in that same city! It all turned out well, but my father not only experienced deep rejection from his family, but missed out on some important years of being fathered.

My dad had no problems with his masculine identity. Though he wasn't what is considered "macho," he liked being a man and was confident of his physical prowess. He told me how at the end of World War I when he and a trainload of other soldiers returned to their hometown in Port Huron, Michigan, his family was there to meet him.

The soldiers piled off the train, and when dad saw my mom, he hugged and kissed her, then picked her up and lifted her over his head to celebrate victory! At his grocery store he was known to lift two one hundred-pound bags of grain at the same time, one on each shoulder, so he was pretty strong.

Parents and children always have things to forgive one another for. It works both ways. My father and I had a break in relationship from when I was fourteen until I was twenty-six. This made a deep impact on my life because a girl entering puberty needs her father's love and approval more than ever. So during those years the love and affirmation I should have received from my dad, I got from my girlfriends and boyfriends. My father never approved of any of the young men in my life, and he let them know it, which discouraged them one by one!

In addition to his rejection by his father at seventeen, my dad's sense of self-worth was further damaged because due to the Great Depression, things weren't good financially at the time he came to Florida. As a businessman, he struggled along over the years.

My dad mellowed as he grew older, even as I find myself doing! He had been in a full-gospel church for some years and believed in the experience of the empowering of the Holy Spirit for some time before he actually received it in 1954. Beginning at that time, and in the years following, he was changed from a person of law to one of grace.

Under completely different circumstances, I too received this same experience in 1960, and my life too was transformed. The Lord then could do a work of reconciling us and healing our relationship. So the way I began to receive soul healing with my father was through each of us receiving the power of the Holy Spirit (Acts 1:8). Dad and I were again close friends from then on, and I'm glad to say that he heartily approved of my marriage to Dennis in 1966!

I was with my father when he died in 1979. Toward the end, though in a coma and seemingly unable to speak or move, with supernatural strength he lifted his hands high into the air in order to show he was saying, "Praise the Lord!"

Praying with others for healing with their fathers has helped me understand what happened to me.

1. It's important to understand your woundedness.

2. Then realize what has been lacking in your life as a result.

3. Walk through those memories and feelings with Jesus, forgiving and asking forgiveness where needed.

4. Accept the situation as part of learning, and anticipate discovering how God will turn it to good.

5. Let the past go, live in the now, and look forward to the future.

Getting Rid of Anger With Your Father

You may be angry with your father, perhaps for one or more of the reasons listed at the beginning of this chapter. The higher your expectations, the greater the hurt and then anger. But anger can actually turn to be beneficial. "How?" you may ask. Because it can pinpoint a need.

If you have overreacted angrily to a situation, ask yourself, "Why did I get so angry?" You may see that your anger comes from feeling taken advantage of, or perhaps from being put down. If you see a pattern in your anger, pray and ask God to show you where the feelings came from.

(Many men, in particular, are not in touch with their feelings. They let anger build up and don't defuse it by talking about it, or praying about it, and at some point there in an explosion. Not only are the people closest to them injured, but they themselves are hurt. They may feel shame, or even self-hatred. Also it's unhealthy. Have you ever taken your blood pressure after having a temper tantrum? It will be high, believe me!)

Perhaps you're angry because your father was himself an angry person. An angry man is stuck in the "Hurt Child," in emotional immaturity. Often you will find your anger is rooted in your relationship with your father, perhaps in very early days. If you want to be enabled to forgive him, it helps to realize what your father was like when he was a child. Turn to and pray the "Parent as a Child Prayer" at the back of chapter 5, substituting *father* in place of *mother*.

If your father called you unkind or evil names, pray a Word Replacement prayer as Beth did in chapter 6. If you made an inner vow to get even with with your father, renounce and break that vow as Marty did in chapter 2.

On Forgiving Too Soon

If you were abused or molested by your father, you may need to get release from inner anger which perhaps you're not even aware of. If you continue to repress this anger, one or several things may result:

1. Your sexual responses in marriage may be negatively affected.

2. You may find yourself doing to another what was done to you.

3. You may become a "rescuer" going around trying to "save" everyone in need.

Some therapists, secular and Christian alike, warn against forgiving too quickly, before you have expressed your anger. This applies especially where abuse or molesting has gone on for a long time. If you forgive too quickly, they believe, you will be likely either to repress your real feelings and/or will feel guilty.

I agree you should not be superficial in dealing with your anger, but on the other hand, as the Apostle Paul says, you should not "let the sun go down on your wrath" (Ephesians 4:26). To me this means that by the end of each day you need, with God's help, to forgive and be forgiven.

Two Kinds of Forgiveness

How can this paradox be reconciled? How can you forgive right away, and yet take time to get in touch with your deep feelings? By soul-healing prayer you can do both. You can forgive *with your will* immediately, or at least by the end of each day, and then forgive deeply *with your emotions* from the past, taking time to do this, perhaps over a period of years.

Prayer with Beth is an example of forgiving both ways: in the present, and from the time frame of the original hurts. She forgave her parents as well as she could from her present will, and then you've followed her as she forgave: before birth, at birth, ages three, nine, ten, eleven, twelve, and so on, wherever the healing was needed.

Forgiving daily with your will is vital for your protection in spiritual warfare. (A "wish I wanted to" prayer would work here. See chapter 5.) Living and walking in the darkness of unforgiveness leaves you vulnerable to "fiery darts" of the enemy. Scripture says that forgiving and being forgiven helps you "walk in the light as He is in the light" (1 John 1:7,9). It keeps you in right relationship with God and under the protection of the blood of Jesus.

So you should honestly tell God, while alone or with someone helping you, about the anger you feel with your parent, and get it out in the open. Then you can go on to pray for inner healing, so you can *forgive him more deeply from your emotions, over a period of time.*

As you pray through each memory (see the prayers at the end of this chapter) and know that God has healed you, you will be enabled to forgive. Finally, you need to ask God's forgiveness for your anger.

To illustrate, let me tell you about a phone call I received recently. I had met a new friend at church and she had phoned to discuss getting together to pray. She told me, "I'm a compulsive eater. I've had two stomach staplings, which I've blown by gorging myself, and even had intestinal bypass surgery. You wouldn't believe all I've done to my body to try to lose weight! With the Holy Spirit's help, I've now gone from 342 pounds to 202. I'm presently a member of the Overeaters Anonymous, which is excellent support, but my compulsion is still here.

"I know my basic problem," she continued, "is that I'm not ready to forgive my mother. I really don't want to love her because if I do, I'm afraid I'll be vulnerable to more hurt."

I said to her, "You've already forgiven your mother and everyone across the board this morning at Holy Communion when you prayed the prayer of Confession of Sins.[1] You've forgiven her with your will, which places you under God's protection. If you hadn't done this you wouldn't have worthily received from the Lord's Table."

"I never thought of it that way," she replied.

I went on, "Now when we meet together for prayer, we'll help you forgive from your emotions. You won't have to do this all at once, but over a period of time, and with God's healing power, you will be able to forgive fully."

"Oh, that gives me such comfort," she said.

(What applies to mothers, of course, applies to fathers, too.)

This is the value of being able to forgive two ways: one immediately, the other over a period of time. The first is forgiving on the level of your relationship with God. The second is forgiving on the level of your relationship with man (if you cannot verbalize *this* forgiveness it shows you still have emotional blocks). The first cleanses you in your relationship to God. The second releases you in your relationship to people. One is necessary to salvation. The other is not, but is a powerful tool to make you more open toward God and man. One is forgiving on the level of your spirit, your will being the doorway from soul to spirit. The second is forgiving from the level of your soul (emotions, memory, and will).

Praying About Molestation

If you need to pray about having been molested by a parent or substitute parent, get two experienced prayer-counselors to help you. *Don't tackle it alone.*

There are exceptions. A man I know of read my book *Emotionally Free* while in a penitentiary cell with several other men. He decided he needed to pray about the memory of having been molested. None of his companions were likely prayer partners, and he had no privacy, so he plugged his ears and blindfolded his eyes. He prayed, and was healed!

As a last resort I suggest that if you have no one nearby who has experience in soul-healing prayer, you find two Spirit-filled Christians who are interested in helping you, and are willing to read my first book, as my prisoner friend did, as well as *How to Pray for Inner Healing*. Then go ahead and pray. The Lord will lead you, as you follow the instructions in the books. You'll probably want to meet for prayer several times. You'll know when you're healed.

Note please! In prayer for memories about being molested, you should not try to relive the experience itself, but come into the memory only where and when you are aware of God's Presence and can receive His comfort. The Holy Spirit will direct you. Then forgive the person or persons who hurt you, from the time it happened. In some instances misplaced anger at God will need to be dealt with before you pray about the memory.

In the Lord's Prayer, master of all inner-healing prayers, Jesus teaches that by the same measure you forgive, you are forgiven. The surest way to bind your emotions is not to forgive. That little child within you is being forgiven and set free as he forgives. Even if he couldn't do it earlier, he/she can do it now.

Whether or not your situation involved any of the four forms of abuse (*see* chapter 5) including sexual abuse, in prayer Jesus can be the channel to give you a father's love. Jesus is God the Son. That means He did not come into being when He was born on this earth; He has always existed. He has always been with His Father.

When He came on His mission to earth to save the human race, God the Father was with Him and in Him, "Reconciling the world unto Himself." Jesus practiced His Father's Presence. ". . . I am not alone, because the Father is with Me" (John 16:32).

Even if you didn't have an earthly father's love, in addition to His own love, Jesus can give you a Father's love—His own Father's love.

And that's what I want you to look at in more detail in the concluding chapter . . .

Soul-Healing Preparation, Prayers, Evaluation, Additional Thoughts

Preparation. In the prayer that follows, you are going to let the Holy Spirit show Jesus with you in scenes which to you are in the past, but are present to Him who is everywhere present.

This is what I call a "Reliving the Hurt Memory" or "Reliving the Scene With Jesus" prayer. This means, with Jesus as your omnipresent Lord, you go to a hurting place in your memories, coming into it *where Jesus leads You,* and relive it, appropriating His healing love. You tell Him how you feel, how you hurt. You listen to Him as He speaks words of comfort, gives you insight into yourself and others in the situation, and then you take time to rest in His healing Presence. When ready, and with the Lord helping, you forgive those who injured you, and if any of your own attitudes were wrong, ask God's forgiveness from this scene of your past.

You have read and complied with the prayers in Appendixes A and B, and are ready to begin.

Ask the Holy Spirit to show you what to pray about. (If you are working through a memory of sexual molestation, be sure to have experienced prayer counselors, or a Christian therapist who practices inner-healing prayer, work with you.) As the Spirit of God brings a memory to your mind, realize Jesus was there with you and let the Holy Spirit show Him to you in the scene. He was present when the hurt took place, but wasn't able to help for several reasons:

First, because in this fallen world good and bad people alike have been given free will, and Jesus will not take away this freedom. Some people will use their freedom of choice for good, and some for evil.[4]

Second, the hurt may have been before you knew Jesus, so you didn't know you could call on Him for help.

Third, it may have taken place when you were too young to know your authority in Christ and claim it.

Reliving Hurtful Memories With Jesus Prayer. Begin like this:

Lord, I cast down all vain or useless imaginations and every high thing that exalts itself against the knowledge of God. Through Jesus, I pull down strongholds and bring into captivity every thought to the obedience of Christ. In all my ways I acknowledge You so You can direct my paths. (*Personalized from 2 Corinthians 10:5 and Proverbs 3:6.*)

Jesus was there with you, and hurt when you hurt. Now allow Him to be Lord of that past event, so He can do and say what He originally wanted to in order to heal your wounded emotions. Be expecting Him to guide you and help you see situations and people through His eyes. Let the Holy Spirit show you Jesus as He is, unconditionally loving. He's your best friend and you're God's child. Take some time to see what memory God wants to heal for you now. (*Pause here for the Lord's direction.*)

As we follow the scriptural admonition to "seek His face," which means to seek His Presence, we experience Him in a variety of ways, perceiving Him "after the Spirit." Some are blessed with a vision of Jesus when they pray. Some people when they pray do not see Jesus, but they just *know* He is there. They know that He has compassionate eyes, a loving smile, strong hands with nail scars in them which show His love for us all.

Can you imagine how His voice sounded when He talked to His followers: to the little boy with the loaf of bread and fishes; to Mary Magdalene when He called her name; to the children when He called them to come to Him; to Peter when He gave him a new name? He must have a wonderful laugh, for Scripture says His Father anointed Him with joy above all His friends (Hebrews 1:9). Perhaps He'll call your name. Listen to His voice and see how beautiful it sounds. He said, "My sheep hear My voice, and I know them, and they follow Me" (John 10:27). (*Pause.*)

If you are unable to see Jesus in the scene, or even sense that He is there, ask yourself what He would have said and done if He had been allowed to help you.

(*Pause here, and wait on the Lord.*)

Wherever you can identify with Jesus in your hurts, do so. Ask Him what it was like if He was hurt in a similar manner. Prayer is talking to God and then taking time to listen to Him. Let your inner child have a voice to talk to Him now. Tell Him how you feel in this memory. (*Pause and express your feelings to God.*)

The first key to soul healing is *God's unconditional love.* Jesus brings peace and joy, and He loves you with total love. Though He knows your every imperfection, He accepts you as you are. You are special to Him. Listen to His words of love and affirmation. Pray the words the child Samuel was taught to pray, ". . . Speak Lord, for your servant hears. . ." (1 Samuel 3:9). Let Jesus be to you, and do for you, what you needed most at this time. (*Take time to hear and receive from the Lord. Whatever you receive must be in agreement with Scripture and the loving, and holy nature of God.*)

Now speak as from the age you were when the hurt occurred. If you were six, speak as from your six-year-old self and offer forgiveness to your father or others who may have been there at the time. Forgiveness is offered as in the past and as to the people who were there at that time. This can happen through Jesus, for all times are present to Him. Forgive from your feelings of the past:

"Through Jesus I forgive you, Dad. What you did hurt me [*take time to express your feelings here*], but I will not hold onto this hurt any longer. Jesus has set me free to forgive and love you, Dad. I forgive you for not being to me what I needed you to be."

Evaluation. (*If you felt blocked when you began to pray, check to see if you have forgiven your parent "across the board" with your will. Don't overlook this.*)

If you find *you* too have sinned through a wrong reaction to a hurt, or for some other reason, pray, "Dear Father God, please forgive me for (*name it*). I truly repent and I'm sorry. By Your grace, Lord, I will allow You to change me and make me more like Jesus. Thank You, Lord, that Your Blood has cleansed me. In Jesus' name I pray. Amen."

First John 1:9 says: "If you confess your sins, God is faithful and just to forgive your sins and to cleanse you from all unrighteousness" (paraphrased). God's Word proclaims you are forgiven. Praise Him for it. (*If you need more assurance of forgiveness, see your minister or priest.*)

The only way to get rid of *real guilt* is through repenting and receiving God's forgiveness. An effective way to get rid of *false guilt* is through soul (inner)-healing prayer. False guilt refers to things you've repented of but didn't forgive yourself for, or things others blamed you for which you didn't do.

(*Take some time to praise the Lord for what He's done for you. Later jot down some notes in your prayer journal.*)

You Can Also Relive Some Happy Memories With Jesus. After praying for healing of past hurts, call to mind if you can, some good things that happened with your parent, and walk through them with Jesus.

Or you may want first to remember some happy memories with you and Jesus alone.

1. *Ask the Holy Spirit to show you a place where Jesus was with you during your childhood.* Go there in prayer and experience His Presence.

When Sheila Todd, a friend of mine, prayed this way, the Lord reminded her of a time early in childhood when she got her first Bible and carried it around with her everywhere she went, even to public school. Though she could only read one phrase of Psalm 23: "The Lord is my shepherd," she read it over and over.

2. *Remember the first person you ever felt loved you in your childhood or as a young adult, and experience Jesus there with you.*

3. *Recall when you first accepted Jesus, or think of when you were baptized as a baby or as a young person.* Relive that memory with Jesus.

4. *Remember a childhood activity such as your favorite hobby, indoor or outdoor games, and recognize that Jesus was there with you to enjoy that time with you.*

Whether you pray alone or with another person, the Holy Spirit will guide you to do what's needed, where to begin and where to end. (*Take some time here to pray.*)

Chapter Nine

Peace With Your Heavenly Father

FATHER'S DAY

Most important in a child's world is his father,
Because a father either points a child to God
or away from Him.
You are a reflection of what your children believe God to be.
Let your light so shine that they will see God in you
And glorify your Father in Heaven.

RITA BENNETT, Based on
Proverbs 17:6, 1 Corinthians 11:7, Matthew 5:16

Healing of the earthly father relationship is one of the greatest tools of evangelism, because our picture of God is based on it. Those with a good earthly father (or strong father substitute) usually come to Jesus more easily. Unless your inner child has been healed, you will see God as you saw your earthly father.

Those with a poor experience of earthly fathering will often strongly resist the idea of the heavenly Father. To such people you could quote Bible verses without end, telling of the love and joy of knowing God, and they still will not accept Him. You will get further, if you want to bring men and women into God's kingdom, by first learning how to pray to get those negative relationships healed.

After hearing me teach about the importance of the father relationship, a man who looked as though he was in his early sixties said to me, "Maybe this is the reason my son has never accepted God. You see, I divorced his mother when he was a little boy and remarried soon after. I rarely saw my son when he was growing up. I've asked the *Lord* to forgive me for my mistakes and sins," he said, "And I'm sure He did, but I've never asked my *son* to forgive me. I'm going to write him a letter to ask his forgiveness. Perhaps that will open the way for him to come to God!"

If you're afraid of your Father God,

or don't feel He loves you,

or have a hard time feeling His Presence,

or feel condemned when you read certain parts of the
Old Testament,

explore these four avenues if you haven't done so already:

1. *Is your wounded inner child confusing your earthly father with your heavenly Father, causing you to resist loving Him or to rebel against Him?*

2. *If you've asked Jesus, who is the Way to the Father, to come into your life, have you allowed the Father to show you what Jesus means when He says, "He that has seen Me has seen the Father?"* (see John 14:6, 9).

3. *Have you received the Baptism or release of the Holy Spirit?* (Acts 1:8). Many, my husband Dennis included, say they began to know the heavenly Father in a new way after they had received this experience.[1]

4. *Have you prayed for healing from hurts with your earthly father?*

What Your Heavenly Father Is Like

Prisons are full of unfathered men and fatherless men. Some mental institutions do not use the Lord's Prayer at chapel services because it begins with "Our Father" and that has such a negative connotation for many of the patients. Yet many churches still paint a picture of our Father in heaven as Someone to be afraid of, Someone you'd want to stay away from as long as possible!

I'd like to quote from an article Dennis wrote in 1983 for our publication *The Morning Watch:*

Father can be a threatening word, and for many "God the Father" seems threatening, a Ruler absolute and arbitrary, like the Queen in *Alice,* ready to say "off with your head" at the least provocation, or without any provocation at all.

. . . If my father disapproved of me, I'll probably feel God disapproves of me too. If my father was brutal and unfeeling, I will be inclined to think of God as brutal and unfeeling. If my father was warm and loving, that's how I will tend to think of God the Father. This is "in the natural." In the spirit I know God loves me, that He is a perfect Father, but the "natural" picture often overwhelms the spiritual one.

Jesus says He is just like His Father. He is the "exact expression" of the Father (Hebrews 1:3). Jesus said, "He who sees Me sees Him who sent Me," and that only through Himself could anyone know or come to the Father (John 12:45).

It's taken some of us a long time to realize we have a good and loving Father in Heaven. But what is a *good* father like? A good father will never stop loving you although He may not approve of everything you do. He'll never disown you, no matter what. If you rebel and run away, a good father will receive you back when you are ready to come.

But there's more to having a father. When you were young, if you were doing things your father didn't approve of, if he really loved you, he didn't just let you go on doing it. Permissiveness, letting kids do whatever they want, is not a sign of love, and kids don't interpret it that way, either. They know very well that when their parents keep them under control, and let them know the limits, they are expressing love to them.

God is not a permissive parent, but He is a perfect parent. He won't let you get away with anything that might lead to your spiritual destruction. If you walk in the devil's territory, God will not stop him from attacking you, but God will not let him destroy you.

Our Father isn't going to overlook our orneriness and meanness. He isn't going to spoil us by letting us go on being as bratty as we want to be! A true father is strict—but he's fair about it. He's going to correct us when we need correcting, but not when we *don't* need it . . .

You have a real Father in Heaven who loves you; one you can talk to whenever you need, and who wants the best for you. When allowed, He'll move Heaven and earth to give you those good gifts and blessings. Yes, and sometimes correction, in love.

Our Father in Heaven is great beyond imagining, high and lifted up, adored by cherubim and seraphim. There are times when we will just want to be praising Him. But He is also truly our Father; we have been adopted into His family.[2]

God the Supreme Affirmer

The Gospels chiefly present God as an affirming Father. When Jesus was beginning His public ministry, just after He was baptized by John the Baptist at the river Jordan, His Father spoke from heaven.

". . . This is my Son, whom I love; with him I am well pleased." (Luke 3:22 NIV)

On the Mount of Transfiguration the Father affirmed Jesus again in the same way (Matthew 17:5; Luke 9:35).

Human fathers should take a lesson from the greatest of all Fathers and learn to affirm their children privately and publicly. You may find this hard to do for your kids if your father didn't do it for you, but you can learn with practice!

Our daughter-in-law Diane, when in her teens, was awakened one night by God speaking to her in an audible voice, calling her by name. She was spontaneously filled with the Holy Spirit, and began to praise Him in the Spirit! What an affirmation that was!

This probably hasn't happened to many others in just this way, but God knew it would be important to Diane to receive this kind of affirmation from Him.

Your heavenly Father and His Son are supreme Affirmers and you can, through prayer, and by meditating on these accounts in the Gospel, receive from God the affirming love you need for your own wholeness. Jesus received affirming love from His Father; let Him pass it on to you. Allow the Lord to show you those scenes where you should have been affirmed and let Him give you the affirmation He wanted you to have.

If your father not only failed to affirm you, but definitely rejected you, you will need more healing prayer, but your hurts can be cured.

The Greatest Story of a Father's Love

"If you rebel and run away, a good father will receive you back when you are ready to come." That's the theme of the greatest story in the Bible on the Father's love. We call it the "prodigal son" (Luke 15:11-32). *Prodigal* means "recklessly extravagant." The son was recklessly extravagant with his father's money but the story might better be called the "Prodigal Father." The father was "prodigal," recklessly extravagant—with his love; and that is the main point of the parable. Jesus knew we'd have more difficulty identifying with the Father whom we had not seen, than with the Son who came to earth as a Human Being, "God made flesh."

Most of you will know the story well. A father had two sons. The younger son took his inheritance and went to a far-off country, squandered all his money in "riotous living," and ended up as a swineherder, sleeping in the pigpen, and eating pig's food. He finally came to his senses and returned home to ask for a job as a laborer on his father's farm. Instead of rejecting him, or punishing him for his actions, his father—a representation of the heavenly Father—showed nine loving acts toward his son:

He saw him while he was still a long way off and felt loving pity for him, ran to meet him, hugged him and kissed him, accepted his repentance without a word of blame, put the best robe on him, put a ring on his hand, put new shoes on his feet, restored him to the family, and made a great feast, with music and dancing.

"The ring and the sandals were marks of a free man, and of honor and dignity (Genesis 41:42; 1 Kings 21:8; Esther 8:2; Daniel 6:17; James 2:2). Formerly captives had their shoes removed (Isaiah 20:2), and when they were liberated their shoes were restored," it says in *Dake's Annotated Reference Bible.*

There are many things you can learn from Jesus' parable, but the key message is that the Father wants His children to come home from their wanderings, and when they do, He loves them and forgives them, restores them to the family, and invites them to share in His joy and glory . . .

Soul-Healing Preparation, Reflection, Evaluations, and Prayer

Preparation. Your imagination is a gift from God and it can be a great inspiration if you place it under the direction and influence of the Holy Spirit. Have you ever imagined how it would be if you had been with Jesus during His earthly life: at His birth; when He fed the multitudes; when He healed the man born blind; when He rose from the dead? *Lectio divina* is one ancient way of reading Scriptures, in English, "holy reading." This means to slowly and prayerfully read and think deeply about God. You can do this with a passage of Scripture, the Lord's Prayer, or a parable from Scripture you have committed to memory. In our fast-paced living it's important to do what God advises us, "Be still and know that I am God" (Psalms 46:10).

Reflection on the Prodigal Child. Take some time to read or reread Jesus' story in Luke 15:11-32, or get ready to reflect on what you already know of this story of the Father's love.

Can you put yourself in the story?

Were you ever rebellious against your heavenly Father?

Are you now? (All of us have been at some point.)

Maybe you also went to a distant land and, in effect, squandered your inheritance. Maybe hurts in your life turned you from God for a time. Perhaps you thought, *If God is like my earthly father I don't want anything to do with Him.* Perhaps you blamed God for what the enemy was doing, and as a result, separated yourself from God. Maybe you failed in life, in marriage, or in business, and felt no one, not even God, wanted you.

Ask yourself, how was I like the Prodigal Son? Have I been a prodigal son or daughter? What has kept me from my Father's house? from my Father's Presence? (*Pause.*)

What has separated me from my Father? Will I say, "I will arise and go to my Father's house" and say, "Because I have sinned I have stayed away from You Father."

Or, "I will arise and go to my Father's house" and say, "The sins of others against me have kept me from coming to You Father."

Or, I will say, "The hurts from living in a fallen world, and not understanding why things have happened to me as they have, kept me from coming to You Father."

Whatever the cause, don't let anything keep you from coming back to your Father's house. (*Pause.*)

Know that the Father loves you unconditionally, just as the father in the Scripture story. He loves you for *who* you are, not for what you have or haven't done. The important thing is that you want to come back to Him. Think of how the Father loves you. He was willing to allow His Son to give His life so that you could have your sins removed and come into His own family. As the spear went through His Son's side, it went through His own heart, just as you would feel if it were you and your own child. Close your eyes, relax, and let His love be absorbed within your spirit, soul and body. (*Pause.*)

What kind of a road do you see yourself walking down? Is it long and dusty or is it paved? Is it in a wooded area? Are there people or signs along the side of the road, trying to lure you away from your intent to go home? Will you resist?

When you get home will you demand your rights, or will you humbly fit in with your Father's plans?

Who is it running toward you on the road with arms outstretched and joy on His face? What affirmation your Father's Presence brings you! Feel His arms around you as He calls your name. What is He saying? (*Pause.*)

You walk joyfully back to the house with your Father. A feast is prepared. After a good bath, you find waiting for you the very best robe available. What joy you have when you receive the ring and new shoes, showing that you're no longer a slave but God's own child. (*Take some time to praise God for what He's done for you. Wait for a while in His Presence, and see what He may show you further.*)

Evaluation. If you found it hard to apply this parable in a personal way, the following may help.

Some people are more open to God the Son, rather than God the Father. If that's your situation, remember Jesus has always been in loving fellowship with His Father, *so His Father's love is a part of Him.* Ask Him to give you His Father's love as well as His own.

I told in chapter 3 of *How to Pray for Inner Healing,* how during a creative prayer Jay felt Jesus said to him, "I will be a Father to you and you can be My son."

Jesus is not the Father but He can function as a Father to God's children (Isaiah 9:6). Jesus is a Brother to us and has been called, ". . . the firstborn among many brothers" (Romans 8:29 NIV). Yet just as a brother can fill a surrogate role of Father in a person's life, so Jesus sometimes needs to be as a Father to us.

Prayer Separating Pictures of Earthly and Heavenly Father. You may have a negative inner picture of your father which needs to be separated from your concept of your Father in heaven. Scripture says, "For the word of God is living and powerful, and sharper than any two-edged sword, piercing even to the division of soul and spirit . . ." (Hebrews 4:12). Your soulish picture of God may need to be distinguished from the true spiritual picture of God. (This verse is first of all speaking of Jesus the Living Word as you'll see from the context, and it is also speaking of the written Word, the Scriptures. *Also see* Revelation 1:16.)

"Dear God, by the power of Your two-edged sword I claim division between the inner pictures I have of my earthly father and my heavenly

Father. I break any wrong hold upon me which would try to keep me from loving and trusting my Father God. If I've blamed You for what my earthly father has done, I ask Your forgiveness. I claim my freedom to love You fully. Thank You, Lord God. In Jesus' name."

Evaluation Concluded. It is more rare, but some people are more open to the Father than to the Son.

If you have a brother you need reconciliation with, this may be keeping you from feeling close to Jesus. It's the same principle as with the earthly father and heavenly Father.

It's important that this be healed because Jesus is the only way to the Father (John 14:6). Jesus also tells us, "... he who loves Me shall be loved by My Father ..." (John 14:21).

In either of these situations further prayer is in order.

Concluding Thoughts

The purpose of this book is to show you how a number of God's children have, through healing prayer, made peace with themselves, peace with their parents, and peace with God. I hope you have been able to plug yourself in here and there. Some of the cases were more serious than others. I've tried the best I could to allow you to walk with us on these prayer journeys. Most important, I've given *you related prayers and ideas to reflect upon* to help you in your own journey to wholeness.

A newspaper reporter once asked me, "What would have happened to these people if you and your friends had not prayed for them?" In the light of that question I'll answer what isn't certain but seems most probable.

Beth would have ended her life, Martha would have continued in her inner battle with her confused identity, Gloria would have gone on hating her mother, falling into the same pattern of living. And to go back to the cases I cited in my first book on soul healing, *Emotionally Free,* Jim would have remained a depressed and ineffective Christian instead of the leader he is now, Meg would have had her fifth nervous breakdown and been readmitted to the hospital for psychiatric care, Susie would have died from anorexia, Dave's marriage would have broken up and his children would have been without a father, to say the very least.

Thanks be to God this is not how the story ends for any of them! They found Jesus had the answers to their deepest needs.

Others I've prayed with about smaller problems might say, "I have a more peaceful life now that I've been able to forgive [spouse, parents, grandparents, children, neighbors, and so forth]." "I'm not afraid to sleep at night anymore." "I can pray out loud in front of people." "My childhood memories are happy now." "I no longer have to try to control everyone who is close to me." "I love people more and am less critical of them." "For the first time I really feel God loves me." "I'm more confident in social situations." "I have a greater sense of freedom inside." "My little daughter is not afraid to let me out of her sight." "My son isn't tormented by nightmares anymore."

Making peace with your inner child doesn't mean, however, that everyone—family, friends, and outright enemies—will necessarily be at peace with you. Even Jesus, who is the Prince of Peace, didn't experience that. Until Jesus returns to this earth and all things are given into the Father's hands, there will be spiritual warfare going on, but God wants us to have peace even in the midst of battle. That's why spiritual armor for the Christian includes shoes of peace (Ephesians 6:15). No, you can't force people to be at peace with you. What you can do, though, is *be at peace with God and yourself.* That goes a long way toward making peace with the others in your life. Learning to practice living in God's peace isn't always easy, but it is one of the most important things you can do.

Jesus Christ is your peace (Ephesians 2:14). The essential peace, residing in your spirit, comes from meeting and receiving Him. And that, too, is the only place true peace for your soul can be found. Your soul—intellect, will, emotions, memories, subconscious, personality, creativity, motivations—has the potential for total peace, but there may be wounds, some very deep, not yet healed. Each of us will need further healing during our lifetime.

God has made the Way. His Name is the Lord Jesus Christ. Even now, the lion shall lie down with the lamb, and the Child/Man, Jesus, will lead you. The inner child in Jesus can relate to and empathize with the inner child in you. "While You [Father God] stretch out Your hand to cure and to perform signs and wonders through the authority and by the power of the name of Your holy Child and Servant Jesus" (Acts 4:30 AMPLIFIED). Put your hand in the hand of the Holy Child Jesus, and He will bring you wholeness. As you do so, you're also putting your hand in the hand of the resurrected Lord, who, being all knowing and outside the limits of time, understands all about you from conception to the present and beyond, and knows *exactly* how to bring life out of death. You need only to be willing to take the first step to begin to be made whole . . .

> *Finally . . . Become complete.*
> *Be of good comfort,*
> *be of one mind,*
> *live in peace;*
> *and the God of love and peace will be with you.*
>   2 Corinthians 13:11

Appendix A

Prayer for Receiving Jesus

Sincerely pray the following prayer:

Dear Father, I believe Jesus Christ is Your only-begotten Son. I believe He became Man, taking on our human nature. I believe He died on the Cross, and poured out His life's blood to cleanse away the guilt and sin that is separating me from You. I believe He rose from the dead, physically, and that He can give me a new kind of life.

Lord Jesus, I confess my sins to You—all the wrong things I've done, the darkness, the guilt, and the fear in my life—wash them away with Your precious blood. I accept Your forgiveness. I know that You have cleansed me, and set me free. I invite You to come into my life right now. I receive You as my Savior and Lord. Thank You for giving me the Holy Spirit. I'm a child of the Father! I'm born again of the Spirit! I'm a new creature! Thank You, Jesus." (From *Emotionally Free*, p. 72.)

When you prayed this prayer, you may have actually felt something happen, or you may not. Your spirit, which came alive through Jesus Christ, is in a place much deeper than your emotions; therefore, sometimes there will be an emotional response—and sometimes not. Whether you felt anything immediately or not, you have received Him by faith and you will see the results.

Get a Bible and look up these Scriptures: Romans 3:23; Romans

6:23; Romans 5:8-10; John 1:12; Revelation 3:20; Ephesians 2:8, 9; 2 Corinthians 5:17. These verses paint a picture of what God has done for you. Read these and 1 John 5:10-15 each day for two weeks and thank God for salvation. Tell someone what's happened to you. Write down today's date in your Bible and celebrate your spiritual birthday each year!

Appendix B

How to Lead Someone in Renouncing the Cults or the Occult

The term *cult* describes religions or philosophies that do not teach the scriptural picture of God and man. Jesus is presented as one among many teachers and saviors, not as God become Man. One cult teaches that men can become gods. Another teaches that sin and sickness are illusions due to wrong thinking—"error of mortal mind."

The cults do not usually believe sins are forgiven through Jesus' death on the cross. Some teach we must make up for our own sins by living again on this earth in other bodies (reincarnation).

Cults are exclusive, and they believe salvation is not through Jesus but through keeping the teachings of the cult.

Intensely exclusive Christian sects are often classed with the cults. These accept scriptural teachings about Jesus and the forgiveness of sins, but add their own doctrines. One group teaches that Jesus is the only Person in the Godhead; He is Himself the Father, Son, and Holy Spirit. Others teach that in order to be saved, you must be baptized in a certain manner, or must keep Saturday as the Lord's Day. They usually teach there is no salvation outside their ranks, and exercise strong control over their members. If you have belonged to one of these groups, you need to renounce the wrong teachings, and may need deliverance from bondage.

The term *occult* means "hidden," and refers to groups that believe they can contact and manipulate the spiritual world to gain information or power. They usually believe in extrasensory perception (ESP), supposed innate ability to foresee the future (precognition), or to know things that are happening at a distance (clairvoyance or "second sight"). They believe such things as "mind over matter" (psychokinesis or telekinesis), for example, the apparent moving or bending of objects by thought power.

Probably the commonest occult activity today is belief in astrology, that the planets and other heavenly bodies can influence human destiny.

The most dangerous occult practice is spiritualism in any form, the attempt to contact the departed through seances, or in any other way.

The reason the occult is so dangerous is that those who practice it really do contact a spiritual world, the so-called "psychic world," but it is Satan's spiritual world, what Paul calls "the powers of the air," and if a person does this, darkness will come into his mind or soul.

Be sure that you renounce both the cults and the occult before you pray for inner healing, or you may become confused, and also confuse others. (For further information on this see *The Holy Spirit and You,* chapter 4, or *How to Pray for the Release of the Holy Spirit,* Appendix 2. Both of these books are listed in the Bibliography. *See also* Deuteronomy 18:9-14.)

Prayer for Renouncing the Cults and Occult. Dear Father, if I have believed, or read, or taught, or taken part in anything that was contrary to Your Word, or displeasing to You, in Jesus' name I renounce those acts or thoughts, and especially [*here mention the specifics that need to be renounced*]. I promise You I will not engage in these anymore, and that I will destroy any literature, equipment, or symbols associated with these things at my earliest opportunity.

Any spirits associated with any of these, in Jesus' name, I bind you and command you to depart from me and trouble me no more. I renounce you, Satan, and all your works.

Jesus, I confess You as my Lord and I thank You for giving Your life for me. I claim the protection of Your precious blood as I pray. Thank You, Jesus. (From *How to Pray for Inner Healing,* p. 122.)

Pray immediately and ask God to fill you with the Holy Spirit in any areas that have been cleansed: Lord Jesus, I ask You to fill my life with Your Holy Spirit that I may walk with You in Your truth and light. Thank You, Lord, for doing this. In Jesus' name. Amen.

Appendix C

Many Kinds of Prayer

Soul or inner-healing prayer is only one among many kinds of prayer, as they have been named and used by Christian believers through the centuries:

Confession of sins

Meditation—pondering deeply about God and on the Scriptures

Contemplation—beholding God and loving Him

Adoration—actively loving God and praising Him

Intercession—praying for others, making your prayers a channel for God's will to be done

Supplication or Petition—asking God to meet your own needs and those of others

Thanksgiving

Silent prayer—listening to God

I use many of these in my private prayers.

During soul-healing prayer my prayer partners and I use *intercession,* especially when the other partner is ministering. *Contemplation* is used as we look to the Lord our Healer. We often wait *in silence* to receive direction from the Lord and gifts from the Holy Spirit. *Confession of sins* is used as needed.

We will also often pray "in the Spirit," as Paul calls it, allowing the Holy Spirit to give us "words which are not in our power to say" (Romans 8:26 THE NEW TESTAMENT IN BASIC ENGLISH). We praise the Lord at the end of a victorious prayer time, and during the prayers.

This book has suggested ways to pray that may be new to you, but I want to be sure you see that more well-known ways are not being ignored. I do, however, believe Jesus is still teaching us, His modern-day disciples, how to pray. He [Jesus] said to them, "Therefore every teacher of the law who has been instructed about the kingdom of heaven is like the owner of a house who brings out of his storeroom new treasures as well as old" (Matthew 13:52 NIV).

Names given to prayers described in this book are for the purpose of making it easier to talk to you about them. Feel free to use the prayers, but be sure to let God guide you creatively. Don't just reduce them to formulae. The Holy Spirit is the Power behind our efforts, and I've just tried to describe to you how He's been working with us.

Source Notes

Chapter 1   Making Peace With Your
Hurt Inner Child

1. A book, *Trevor's Place*, has been written by Frank Ferrell about Trevor and his charitable activities. Published by Harper and Row Publishers, Inc., 1985.
2. John Powell, S. J., *Why Am I Afraid to Love?* (Allen, Tex.: Argus Communications, 1967), p. 30.
3. An excellent definition of *omnipresence* is found in *The Zondervan Pictorial Bible Dictionary,* general editor Merrill C. Tenney, and published in Grand Rapids, Michigan, 1963, p. 609. "Omnipresence . . . the attribute of God by virtue of which He fills the universe in all its parts and is present everywhere at once. Not a part, but the whole of God is present in every place. The Bible teaches the omnipresence of God (Psalms 139:7-12; Jeremiah 23:23, 24; Acts 17:27, 28). This is true of all three members of the Trinity. They are so closely related that where one is the others can be said to be (John 14:9-11)." There are many more verses of Scripture in the Bible on the omnipresence of God.
4. This is a pseudonym.
5. For further guidance in prayer, you should read the books, *Emotionally Free* and *How to Pray for Inner Healing for Yourself and Others. See* Bibliography.

Chapter 2 Marty Makes Peace With Martha

1. Marty and Martha are pseudonyms made as per request.
2. Exodus, International—North America: "Founded in 1976, Exodus is a Christian organization which seeks to equip and unify agencies and individuals to effectively communicate the message of liberation

from homosexuality . . ." See their publication *The Exodus Standard,* P.O. Box 2121, San Rafael, CA 94912.

3. Axel Ingelman-Sundberg and Claes Wirséns, *A Child is Born* (New York: Reprinted by arrangement with Delacorte Press, Dell Publishing Co., Inc., 1980).

4. "Conventional wisdom holds that children before the age of two do not think and do not feel, therefore it really does not matter how you treat them. Life makes no impact on them—and even if it does, they will not remember it later. This attitude is based principally on outdated neurological findings which showed that the large nerve tracts of the central nervous system did not become myelinized until age two, and consequently, could not function—and to a lesser extent, on Freud's contention that only with the acquisition of language did children begin to use symbols, in other words, 'think' and lay down memories.

"The traditional scientific assumption about the so-called immaturity of the central nervous system before age two is being seriously challenged. The question is no longer whether children can think and feel before they are two years old, but rather how soon after conception can they perceive and feel . . .

"In 1963 Grafstein reported that myelinization was not necessary for function but only aided the speed of conduction along large nerve fibers and tracts. In 1966 Salam and Adams proved that neuronal assemblies begin to function before the appearance of the first myelin. Indeed, according to these investigators, an amazingly complex series of reflex activities begin to appear as early as five weeks after conception . . ."

"Prenatal Psychology: Implications for the Practice of Medicine" by Thomas R. Verny, psychiatrist, author. *Canadian Family Physician,* Vol. 30, October 1984.

5. When Christians who have renounced the cults and occult come together in prayer to practice Jesus' Presence throughout their lives, fearful pictures will not come to mind. For example, let's take the years from 1978 through 1986. During this time Dennis and I trained prayer-counselors for soul healing in churches throughout the USA, parts of Canada, and other countries. Those prayer-counselors have, at our seminars alone (not to mention their continuing ministries afterward), prayed with more than 7,000 people.

Visualizing in prayer (seeing by faith) should be avoided if a Christian is actively engaging in cultic or occult practices, trying to mix his beliefs. The results very likely could be demonic.

My conclusion is this: There are three ways human beings can visualize. Two are acceptable to God, but one isn't.

First, you can visualize in the natural and you do this every day whatever you may be: student, homemaker, teacher, surgeon, artist, or businessman.

Second, as a Spirit-filled Christian you can let God speak to you through pictures as you pray or meditate on His Word, or simply wait upon Him in prayer and praise. This is not something you cause to occur, but He may choose to work this way as you are open to Him.

By Jesus' life and example He shows both of these to be beneficial, and these are experienced in soul-healing prayer.

The third way to visualize, the way which is *not* acceptable, is in the psychic realm—the *wrong* supernatural. This is done by people in the cults and occult, as in transcendental meditation, where they make themselves passively open to any thought or picture that comes to their minds. Or in "out-of-the-body experiences" where, with the aid of breathing techniques, and so forth, people picture themselves leaving their bodies and traveling to other places—so-called astral projection. Another would be in "mind control" techniques.

Satan will attempt to use psychic activities to cast doubt on the value of true supernatural experiences in Christianity, causing some well-meaning people to place them both in the same category. Because Satan will use false signs and wonders doesn't mean Christians should be frightened away from allowing God to work through them in *true* signs and wonders. Faced with the counterfeits of the enemy, Christians must move more in the power and love of God than ever before!

Please note: If you would like more information to clarify questions regarding visualization in prayer, and other topics related to soul or inner healing, write for a free copy of the pamphlet *Questions and Answers to Help Clarify the Ministry of Soul or Emotional Healing.* Please include a stamped, self-addressed envelope. Mail to Christian Renewal Association, P. O. Box 576, Edmonds, WA 98020. You may also write to Dennis and me at this address for information on our speaking itinerary or to obtain a directory of churches that can help you.

6. Those in the ministry of soul-healing prayer would do well to look into the effect alcoholism has on children. This is a subject of increasing interest. A helpful book is *Adult Children of Alcoholics* by

Janet Geringer Woitiz, published in 1983 by Health Communications Inc., Hollywood, Florida 33020.

7. When a woman chooses a masculine name for herself it doesn't always mean she has an identity problem. The motive behind such a name change is the important issue. It could merely be that the woman likes the sound of the new name or that someone else gave it to her as a nickname and it stuck. It's interesting, the effect a person's name has on him or her!

8. In evaluating herself, Marty later wrote, "I tended to be a compulsive caretaker—gravitating toward needy people, so that in nurturing them, I was indirectly giving my hidden child the care she'd never had."

9. The idea of "inner vows" needing to be prayed about did not originate with me. I do not know who to give credit to for the original concept, but it is useful.

Chapter 3 A Gift of Peace for You

1. *The Book of Common Prayer,* 1979, gives a prayer layman can pray after a person has confessed sins. It is, "Almighty God have mercy on us, forgive us all our sins through our Lord Jesus Christ, strengthen us in all goodness, and by the power of the Holy Spirit keep us in eternal life. Amen." A clergyman praying this would substitute "you" for "us" and "your" for "our." (*See* p. 80.)

Chapter 4 Making Peace With Your Inner Parents

1. *See* Dennis Bennett, *Moving Right Along in the Spirit*, chapters 1 and 2 (Old Tappan, N.J.: Fleming H. Revell Company, 1983).

2. This illustration is not being given to say "all movies are good." Although Dennis and I do not have or do not take a lot of time to attend movies, we've felt it necessary to walk out of several of them in the last few years. At the same time, movies like *Chariots of Fire* and *The Gods Must Be Crazy* have encouraged us to believe that the trend may be improving.

3. For help in learning how to pray with others for soul healing see *How to Pray for Inner Healing for Yourself and Others. See* Bibliography.

4. This kind of legalism is what kept many Christians in Germany from rescuing the Jews. Since the Bible said to obey those who have the rule over you, they therefore erroneously believed they couldn't go against Hitler and his atrocities! (Romans 13:1)

5. On the effects of incest, please read "The Incest Legacy—Why

Today's Abused Children Become Tomorrow's Victims of Rape" by Diana E. H. Russell, *The Sciences* magazine, New York Academy of Science, March-April 1986.

Chapter 5 Peace With Your Mother

1. Thomas Verny, M.D. with John Kelly, *The Secret Life of the Unborn Child* (New York: Dell Books, 1982).
2. Credit to my husband, Dennis, for this helpful concept of opening the door to forgiveness.
3. Credit to my good friend and colleague, Shade O'Driscoll, for sharing with me the creative idea of forgiving parents, while picturing them in the role of children.
4. In the Parent as a Child Prayer, we are speaking as from the past. We should always be careful not to seem to speak directly to a person who is no longer alive; that is strictly against God's rules (Deuteronomy 18:10,11; 1 Samuel 28:7-20).
5. While he was attending a conference Dennis and I held in Seattle in 1984, Bill Hernandez of *Love in Action Ministries* was given this inspired idea of receiving a mother's love through Jesus. As Jesus received His mother's love, so He can impart a mother's love to us.

Chapter 6 Beth Makes Peace (Part One)

1. If you want more information on the subject of the triune person, please read *Trinity of Man,* by Dennis and Rita Bennett, published by New Leaf Press, Green Forest, Arkansas, 1987. This information is foundational in understanding the healing of the inner person.
2. Beth went back to college during the years of 1979 to 1981; in 1981 we prayed only twice. In 1983, as friendship with another surrogate mother-figure blossomed, she had fewer needs, and we didn't pray with her at all. By my records, and from the prayer journal I asked Beth to keep, we estimate there have been to date (June 1986) a total of twenty-seven to thirty prayer sessions from two to two and a half hours each time. (Additional social contacts and telephone calls with both Janet and me not included.)
3. Many doctors today are aware of the negative effect words can have on patients, even when they are fully anesthetized.
4. Jesus forgives sins, but different denominations have varying attitudes on how forgiveness is administered and received. Follow the pattern of your own church. If you belong to a denomination such as the Episcopalian or Roman Catholic, which reserves the role of de-

claring forgiveness of sins to someone who has been ordained to the priesthood, then you ought to respect those beliefs and practices. Read words of forgiveness from Scripture: "The Scripture says that if we confess our sins He is faithful and just to forgive us our sins, and to cleanse us from all unrighteousness. You have confessed your sins, so we know God has forgiven you." As you proclaim the Scripture, its truth sets people free.

It is often helpful to lay your hand on the person's head or shoulder while giving this assurance. If your church offers private sacramental confession, and the person you are praying with feels the need for further assurance, encourage him to avail himself of it.

5. We like to have people follow in the *deliverance prayer* so they can learn how to pray for themselves when they need to, without thinking they must have another person to assist them. Any Christian who's in right standing with God can pray for deliverance (James 4:7).

Note we are distinguishing between *deliverance* and *exorcism*. *Exorcism* is prayer for those possessed of the devil, and, if possible, should be carried out by a person who has experience in this ministry. Possession means that the whole person has been taken over by the enemy—spirit, soul, and body. A Christian can be depressed, oppressed, or temporarily invaded *in his soul* if he is not walking with the Lord, or doesn't know about spiritual warfare.

Deliverance means driving away the spirits of the enemy that are oppressing the *soul* of the person. It can be, and usually is a fairly simple and undramatic procedure that any Christian can carry out, either for himself or someone else. It is always best, when praying for deliverance, to have the person pray for him or herself, even if you have to have him/her follow you word for word in the prayer.

6. Rita Bennett, *Emotionally Free* (Old Tappan, N.J.: Fleming H. Revell Company, 1982), p. 126.

7. Dale Douglas Mills, cover story, "Are the Seeds of Suicide Planted During Babyhood?" *The Seattle* (Washington) *Times Magazine,* September 23, 1979.

8. Janet was inspired to see this Scripture in a unique way, and it became a *rhema* or living Word for Beth. In the Scripture referred to, Jesus is speaking to the ancient church of Philadelphia. Before He speaks to them, He describes Himself as the One who has the key of David. (Chapter 1 also says He has the keys of hell and death.)

Chapter 7 Beth Makes Peace (Part Two)

1. Thomas Verny, M.D., with John Kelly, *The Secret Life of the Unborn Child* (New York: Summit Books, 1981), pp. 20, 21. Here Dr. Verny describes the effect of smoking on the unborn child. Such knowledge has helped us know how to pray more effectively. (This book is now available in paperback, published by Dell Books, 1982.)
2. I had heard that a woman could not get pregnant while she was nursing her newborn baby. I checked this with a capable nurse who works with an obstetrician. She told me that while it is true that the hormones which stimulate lactation (milk production) diminish the probability of ovulation during that time, they do not give complete protection.
3. John 12:21; John 20:11-18; Luke 24:13-35; Luke 24:36-43; John 20:19-25; Acts 9:1-20; Revelation 1:15-18.
4. Prayer based on 2 Corinthians 5:16, Proverbs 29:18, 2 Corinthians 3:18, and 1 Chronicles 16:11.

Chapter 8 Peace With Your Father

1. Leanne Payne, *Crisis in Masculinity* (Westchester, Ill.: Crossway Books, 1985), p. 50.
2. Quote from Father John Hampsch, "Healing of Memories" Tapes, Claretian Tape Ministry, P.O. Box 19100, Los Angeles, CA 90019.
3. "Fathers and Daughters," *Fulness* magazine, March-April 1986.
4. Dennis Bennett, *Moving Right Along in the Spirit* (Old Tappan, N.J.: Fleming H. Revell Company, 1983).

Chapter 9 Peace With Your Heavenly Father

1. Dennis Bennett, *How to Pray for the Release of the Holy Spirit* (Plainfield, N.J.: Bridge Publishing, Inc., 1985).
2. "What Does It Mean to Have a Father?" *The Morning Watch*, Edmonds, WA 98020, Summer 1983.

Bibliography

Bennett, Dennis. *Moving Right Along in the Spirit.* Old Tappan, New Jersey: Fleming H. Revell Company, 1983.

Bennett, Dennis and Rita, *Trinity of Man.* Plainfield, New Jersey: Bridge/Logos International, 1979.

Bennett, Rita. *Emotionally Free.* Old Tappan, New Jersey: Fleming H. Revell Company, 1982.

———. *How to Pray for Inner Healing for Yourself and Others.* Old Tappan, New Jersey: Fleming H. Revell Company, 1984.

The Book of Common Prayer. New York: The Church Hymnal Corporation, 1979.

Dake, Finis Jennings. *Dake's Annotated Reference Bible.* Atlanta, Georgia: Dake Bible Sales, 1963.

Ingelman-Sundberg, Axel, and Claes Wirséns. *A Child Is Born.* New York: Reprinted by arrangement with Delacorte Press, Dell Publishing Co., Inc., 1980.

Payne, Leanne. *Crisis in Masculinity.* Westchester, Illinois: Crossway Books, 1985.

———. *The Healing of the Homosexual.* Westchester, Illinois: Crossway Books, 1985.

Powell, John, S.J. *Why Am I Afraid to Love?* Allen, Texas: Argus Communications, 1972.

Tenney, Merrill C. General Editor. *The Zondervan Pictorial Bible Dictionary.* Grand Rapids, Michigan: Zondervan Publishing House, 1971.

Verny, Thomas M.D., with John Kelly. *The Secret Life of the Unborn Child.* New York: Dell Books, 1982.

Vine, W. E. *An Expository Dictionary of New Testament Words.* Old Tappan, New Jersey: Fleming Revell Company, 1966.

Woitiz, Janet Geringer. *Adult Children of Alcoholics.* Pompano Beach, Florida: Health Communications, Inc., 1983.

Articles

Bennett, Dennis. "What Does It Mean to Have a Father?" *The Morning Watch* (Summer 1983): 1, 2.

Mills, Dale Douglas. "Are the Seeds of Suicide Planted During Babyhood?" *The Seattle Times Magazine,* September 23, 1979, pp. 8-10.

Russell, Diana E. H. "The Incest Legacy—Why Today's Abused Children Become Tomorrow's Victims of Rape." *The Sciences* Magazine, New York Academy of Science (March-April 1986):28-32.

Smalley, Gary. "Fathers and Daughters." *Fulness* magazine P. O. Box 79350, Fort Worth, Texas 76179. (March-April 1986):24.

Verny, Thomas R. "Prenatal Psychology: Implications for the Practice of Medicine." *Canadian Family Physician,* Vol. 30, October 1984.

Other Recommended Books

Bennett, Dennis. *How to Pray for the Release of the Holy Spirit.* Plainfield, New Jersey: Bridge Publishing, Inc., 1985.

Bennett, Dennis and Rita. *The Holy Spirit and You.* Plainfield, New Jersey: Bridge/Logos International, 1971.

Dobbins, Richard D. *Your Spiritual and Emotional Power.* Old Tappan, New Jersey: Fleming H. Revell Company, 1984.

Frost, Robert. *Our Heavenly Father.* Plainfield, New Jersey: Bridge/Logos International, 1978.

Tapscott, Betty. *Inner Healing Through Healing of the Memories.* Kingwood, Texas: Hunter Books, 1975.